Basics Of Hospitality

by
Rajat kaushik

Basics Of Hospitality
by Rajat kaushik

Copyright © 2024

All Rights reserved.

No part of this publication may be reproduced, stored in a retrieval system, or transmitted in any form or by any means, electronic, mechanical, photocopying or Otherwise, without the written permission of the publisher.
The author/editor asserts the moral right to be identified as the author/editor of this work.

ISBN: 978-93-62768-75-9

Published by

DOUBLE 9 BOOKS

2/13-B, Ansari Road
Daryaganj, New Delhi – 110002
info@double9books.com
www.double9books.com
Tel. 011-40042856

ABOUT THE AUTHOR

The author comes with enriched experience of 22 years having worked both in India & Abroad in Hotels, Resorts, Airport & Travel and Tourism Industry In brands like Oberois, ITC Hotels, Sarovar Hotels, South Hall Travels (London), and many more. Started initial stage of career from The Oberois New Delhi in the Front Office Department and later Promoted to the Trident Gurgaon, having worked in Front Office Department, Human Resource & Training and moved up the ladder as General Manager and later as Corporate General Manager. Honoured with Doctorate PHd in Hospitality Management from Cambridge University, completed BSc in Hotel Management from NCHMCT, Post Graduate Diploma in Travel& Tourism from IGNOU and MBA in Human Resource & Industry Relations from Sikkim Manipal University.

CONTENTS

Front Office Management 9

Yield and Revenue Management Systems: Applications
and Future Prospects 48

Hospitality Software, Reservation, Property and Revenue
Management Solutions 92

Customer Care and Customer Relationship: Strategic
Management and Support 110

Performance Assessment 121

Food and Beverage Services - Organization 160

Housekeeping – Definition, Role, Responsibilities and Layout 192

Significance of Food Production Department & kitchen
Planning in Hotel Industry 200

Synopsis

"Basics of Hospitality for beginners" is a comprehensive introductory guide tailored for beginners entering the field of hotel management. Covering the fundamental principles of hospitality, customer service, operations, and management techniques, this book serves as a roadmap for individuals seeking to understand and excel in the dynamic world of hospitality.

Key topics covered include

1. Introduction to Hospitality Industry: Provides an overview of the hospitality industry, its evolution, and its significance in the global economy.

2. Hotel Operations: Explores the various departments within a hotel, including front office, housekeeping, food and beverage, sales and marketing, and human resources.

3. Customer Service Excellence: Emphasizes the importance of delivering exceptional customer service and creating memorable guest experiences.

4. Revenue Management: Introduces revenue management strategies to optimize hotel profitability through pricing, inventory management, and demand forecasting.

5. Marketing and Sales: Discusses marketing strategies and sales techniques to attract and retain guests, including online marketing, social media, and customer relationship management (CRM).

6. Financial Management: Covers basic financial principles relevant to hotel operations, such as budgeting, cost control, and financial analysis.

7. Leadership and Team Management: Provides insights into effective leadership styles, team dynamics, and employee motivation to foster a positive work environment.

8. Trends and Innovations: Explores emerging trends and technologies shaping the future of the hospitality industry, such as sustainability initiatives, digitalization, and guest personalization.

With practical examples, case studies, and industry insights, "Basics of Hospitality for beginners " equips aspiring hoteliers with the knowledge and skills needed to embark on a successful career in hotel management. Whether you're a student, entry-level professional, or career changer, this book serves as an invaluable resource for understanding the intricacies of the hospitality industry and navigating its dynamic landscape.

Front Office Management

In hotel business the layout and working of the front office plays a very vital role, hence, hotel-keepers must keep a close watch on the working of the front office management in particular.

All the activities of the hotels in the different parts of the hotel building are broadly distributed in two areas i.e. front office and the back office. In the front office guests are in touch with the hotel staff directly soon after the entry and functions are visible to the are felt only.

The Front Office is the place which handles room reservations, receives the guests and assigns them their rooms. The Front Office not only deals with the above functions but also sees to guest relations and guest comforts. The Front Office also deals with the check out formalities required before the hotel guest finally vacates the hotel room and departs from the hotel.

Reception department is the most important in the front office area, and the reception department differs from one hotel to the other. Guests visiting any hotel invariably have to approach the reception desk for information, assistance and answers to their problems and queries. In a small hotel the reception practically manages the hotel activities. Receptionists in small hotels will have to act as secretary to the proprietor as well. Reception is the eye and ear of the hotel establishment.

SEQUENCE OF RECEPTIONIST'S TASKS

- Receives guests and checks booking information
- Checks registration
- Gives room
- Inform other departments
- Opens bill
- Notes guests expenditures
- Hand over mail, messages and morning calls, room service orders
- Prepares bills
- Receiving payments

- Notifies departments about departure of guests
- Takes back vacant and ready room

FRONT OFFICE STAFF

Front Office Staff are vital in the sense that they are required to handle all the formalities of reservation, registration, departure etc. of the guest right from the time guest steps in the hotel. They are also required to handle the guest complaints, public relation and liaison works with other departments of the hotels.

In very large hotels, the staff distribution for the front office job may be described in the following pattern.

Orders come from the top to downwards and the accountability and reporting moves upwards. Front Office manager reports to the general manager or proprietor cum manager of the hotel whichever is applicable.

In small hotels the above elaborate organisation does not exist. The receptionist or the supervisor in the reception counter often performs multiple functions within the counter in his or her specified working hours. A model organisation for the front office may be chalked out as under:

QUALITIES OF FRONT OFFICE STAFF

The Front Office Staff have a very demanding role to play in the Hotel. The job calls for tact, diplomacy and communication skills, besides thorough knowledge of their job. An efficient and effective Front Office Staff should keep the following points in mind:

1. Posture-always stand straight, never turn your back to the customer, never lean on the wall or the counter.

2. Patience

3. Tactfulness.

4. Politeness.

5. Honesty in dealings with colleagues, guests and with the organisation.

6. Punctuality

7. Knowledge about the job, place of work, organisation, who is who, places of interest in and around [city], country, etc.

8. Communication skill—verbal and non-verbal.

9. Salesmanship—ability to sell the advantages of the hotel.

10. Keep workplace always neat and orderly.

11. Try to obtain guest feedback.
12. Ability to get along with all types of customers.
13. Intra-personnel, inter-department relationship should be smooth.
14. Relate customer faces with names and remember their likes and dislikes [Personalized service]
15. keep clerical work updated and to the minimum.
16. Never gossip with customers.
17. Refrain from making any personal comment.
18. Keep personal calls to a minimum.
19. Be precise and to the point.
20. Avoid words like I think, I guess, may be, etc. your answers are important to the customer.
21. Voice modulation and speech clarity.

Complaint Handling

There are following categories of Complaints:

(i) Mechanical Complaints: Concern problems with heating, lighting, power, room furniture, door keys, plumbing, TV sets, swimming pool, elevator etc.

(ii) Staff Attitude Complaints are those made by guests against staff attitude. These usually cover insult to guests, careless comments, careless responses, tactless statements, overhearing conversation or overfriendly attitude.

(iii) Service Problems: Such as long waiting time for guests, lack of assistance with luggage, untidy rooms, telephone difficulties, wake up call errors, F & B delivery & quality problems, not getting room supplies.

(iv) Unusual Problems: These relate to lack of public transportation in the area, timing of bar, weather i.e. temperature, etc.

Surfacing Common Complaints

One of the easiest ways to determine what guests complain most often in a hotel is to ask each employee in the Front Office to make a list of most frequent complaints. Another method is to collect and analyse guest comments through a questionnaire. The guest questionnaire can be posted at the front desk or when the guest is checking out. They can be even placed in rooms or mailed to guests in follow-up letters.

Complaint Handling

The following points need to be borne in mind when handling complaints from Hotel guests.

(a) Listen with concern and courtesy

(b) Never argue with the guest, nor raise your voice,

(c) Try to show maximum amount of interest.

(d) Never go alone to a guest room.

(e) Some guests will never be satisfied and no amount of effort by hotel employees will satisfy them. The hotel's policy regarding these people should clearly spell out what actions are to be taken e.g. initial appeasement efforts refer to supervisors, or perhaps even call the hotel security or civil authorities.

(f) Some complaints are unsolvable. If nothing can be done by the hotel, an admission to the fact or an apology should be made by a hotel representative. A reasonable guest will usually accept an explanation.

METHODS OF HOTEL RESERVATION

Reservation through Telephone

It is quick and gives the receptionist the opportunity to clarify any necessary points about payments, arrival time and so on.

Reservation through Telex

Most larger hotels now have a telex in the reservation department There is less opportunity for misunderstanding because of telex. Another important advantage of the telex in reservation department is that a message can still be sent even though there is no-one on duty at the other end. This is particularly important for hotels with an international clientele. A guest may book from Australia or America without having to check time to ensure that someone will be available to take the reservation. Equally the hotel can telex back a confirmation at any time it wishes.

Reservation through Letter

A letter of reservation is useful because the customer can explain the hotelier when he will be arriving and any special requests he may have. If the guest wishes to charge the account to his company then this can be mentioned in the letter. The hotel in turn can verity if necessary.

Reservation through Computer

An increasing number of hotels are installing computers in their reservation department. This enables contact to be made very quickly with any other group hotel anywhere in the world. Normally the computer information is updated by each unit, and the programme is set so that if one hotel is full it will automatically offer the closest alternative. With these systems the updating of reservation is quick and wide.

Reservation through Personal Contact

Here there is direct face to face contact between the customer and the receptionist. Return bookings are frequently made in this way as a guest depart at the end of his stay. The receptionist has the opportunity to find out the maximum information and can answer any queries the guest have. At times the receptionist may also be able to show the guest the room type and utilise some sales techniques to the potential customers.

Recording the Reservation

Record work should be out of the sight of guest and the reception desk should look neat, clean and tidy.

Reservation Form

Telephone and personal bookings are normally noted on a reservation form. The use of a form for this purpose has many benefits.

Advantages of Reservation Form

1. Acts as a permanent record.

2. Summary of information in a standard format.

3. It acts as a prompt sheet.

4. Running check in progress.

5. Enables the management to find out who took the reservation.

6. Helps in marketing strategies and sales promotion strategies.

CONTENTS OF RESERVATION FORM

Format of Reservation form differs in hotels, but it mostly contains following informations:

1. Name of the guest.

2. Address and Designation.

3. Arrival-Date and Time.

4. Mode of Arrival.

5. Room type.

6. Room Rate.

7. Departure—Date and Time.

8. Booked by i.e. Source of reservation.

9. Name, Address and phone number of the person who booked the room.

10. Billing instructions.

11. Status.

Some hotels combine the reservation form with the Registration Card on the other side so that all the relevant information is available together.

Confirming Reservations

Hotels in india usually confirm the reservation if some advances are taken against booking. Otherwise only large hotels confirm by sending letters, telegram or telex. As individual letters of confirmation become more expensive, some hotels use a standard letter of confirmation to guest booking accommodation.

Cancellation of Reservation

If a guest cancels the booking, then the reservation procedure has to be reversed; the booking is crossed through in the diary the chart entry is erased. The hotel may ask the guest for loss if the guest cancels the booking after contracting but the hotel must make every attempts to sell the room promptly among the wait-listed guests or even to chance guests if available. Apart from the above broad procedure, hotels formulate some policies to organise the total guest arrivals, last minute cancellations, V.I.P. booking etc. These days many hotels have to handle room reservation for guests from delayed or cancelled flights in odd hours with short notice Airlines Company. Hotel also devices own policy for 'Group bookings' by the tour operator on their mutually agreed terms and conditions

Registration

There is a legal obligation in some countries for a hotel to obtain and keep for twelve months, certain information about every person who stays there. The basic requirement is full name and nationality. If the guest is from overseas then they have to fill in additional form.

In addition to this, hotel requests further information from guests sometimes who stay with them. A home address and signature are asked for in all hotels. Others take the opportunity to find out more about their customers by asking information such as purpose of visit, occupation, proposed method of payment and other details. These requests are for administrative purposes to ensure the smooth efficient running of the operation and marketing-where the hotel takes the opportunity to find out more about its customers habits.

Guest Register

The age old method of checking in guests is to use a register. This is a bound book ruled into column which the guest fills out 011 arrival. It is ideal for smaller hotels where guests arrive individually. A register provides a permanent record of guests staying in the hotel.

For efficient and effective working of the hotel some basic documents are to be prepared. The suggested formats of these documents are as follows:

REGISTRATION CARD FORMAT

CONVENTIONAL CHART FOR ADVANCE LETTING CHART

Check the Recorded Information

The receptionist should always check the registration card or registration book once the guest has checked in to make sure that the card has been completed correctly and if there is a query the receptionist can politely ask the guest for clarification. The receptionist can then inform the guest of the room number and the room rate. However, a receptionist must see the following carefully before allotment of room to the guest.

(a) that the registration details are correct and legible.

(b) that the details of the booking have not changed.

(c) that the guest knows the room rate and what it includes.

(d) whether there are any letters or messages for the guest.

(e) that the room is clean and ready in all aspects.

(f) that guest has no bad records and is not black listed.

It is often noticed that guests are allotted the room on the basis of vacancy information only without ascertaining the actual 'readiness' of the rooms. This happens particularly in hotels where there is little time between guest departures and guest arrivals. In such cases the receptionist must tactfully handle guests without annoyance to them to allow time to the housekeeping department to make room ready. But the guests who have booked their hotels in advance must not be kept waiting for their rooms to become ready under any circumstances. A careful and vigilant receptionist must take suitable decisions. It is also important to tackle things at the reception when a guest desires to overstay and the hotel is otherwise booked.

STATUS OF HOTEL ROOMS

A prime need for every hotel reception is an accurate, up-to-date knowledge of the state of every room in the hotel. Hotel room may be in one of the stages as under:

(a) Occupied

(b) Vacant but not ready

(c) Vacant and ready

(d) Under renovation/repair (not fit for occupation)

(e) Vacant but needs urgent attention for fault rectification

(f) Vacant and record but not occupied

(g) Occupied but needs attention for some fault.

A room status system must show these positions for handling guest reservation properly and to organise the quantum of saleable rooms.

Room Allocation

When the guest arrives he will want to be able to use his room as quickly as possible. If he arrives at unscheduled time, it is unlikely that the room will be ready unless it is vacant from the previous night. In smaller hotels allocation of rooms is normally done at the time of booking. Larger hotels with a greater choice of rooms often do not allocate until the guest actually arrives and then place the guest in the room. V.I.P/s and guests with special requirements may have rooms pre-allocated to them and a note may be placed in the reception area to ensure that they only go to those particular rooms. In allocating rooms the receptionist should satisfy the guests as much as possible.

Arrival List

In large hotels this list will be useful to both the hall porter and the telephone operator. The porter or enquiry desk will have to check if there are any messages or letters for guests arriving and the telephone operators answer enquiries from people about the arrival of particular guests. The reception desk will be able to use the alphabetical list to locate guests quickly in the diary,

Departmental Notification

Shifting from one room to another requires an individual notification. Because the records of each department need to be up dated as soon as possible. A format of notification regarding change of rooms is shown in the following:

GUEST MOVEMENT NOTIFICATION FORMAT

Guest Arrivals without Prior Reservation

A guest who comes at the hotel without a prior booking is often referred to as a chance guest. Transit' hotels located near-by station, airports, seaports will receive the bulk of their guests as chance arrivals. The receptionist has practically to information about the guests and the backgrounds. In this situation, special procedures are adopted to handle their bookings.

Chance arrivals with substantial amounts of luggage are unlikely to be able to leave the hotel without paying. An increasing trend, however, is carrying of small amounts of luggage which means the guest may be able to leave unnoticed. In registering the guest, the receptionist first checks whether they have luggage. If they have, then the registration is processed in the normal way and the registration card is marked 'Chance'. If there is little or no luggage then the receptionist has to ensure that the guest will not leave without first settling his or her bill. This can be done either by taking cash deposit from the guest, or alternatively by taking an imprint of any credit card that the guest may have. It is important that in accepting chance bookings and taking deposits, the receptionist does not suggest to the guest that the hotel thinks he/she may be dishonest, or not willing to pay.

Chance guests are often asked to pay cash for all purchases while they are in the hotel, or alternatively a special checks may be kept on the size of their bill so that if the account exceeds some figures, the guest is contacted and asked to make up-to-date payment to minimise the chances of loss.

Over Booking System

This is also known as occupancy management. It is the aim of any hotel to maximise the room occupancy. Many hotels work on the principle of accepting a percentage of more reservations than there is accommodation available. To determine exactly the percentage of more reservation that can be taken a policy of over booking has to be developed. This is done to overcome the problem of no shows, late cancellations, or early departures.

The operating efficiency thus achieved, outweighs the inconvenience to guests and travellers and meets the organisation's financial objectives. The average no-show rate in most of the market is 5 per cent to 15 per cent. Overbooking is worked out as per the following formula.

Where

NA — Non Arrivals

ED — Expected departures

C — Cancellations

OS — Over stays

WI — Walk Ins

TYPES OF REGISTRATION RECORD

(1) Book Bound Register

Normally found in small hotels.

Advantages

(i) All records are available in one book.

(ii) No filing is required.

(iii) Minimum wastage of time and paper.

Demerits

(i) Only one guest checks in at a time.

(ii) Bulky, hence difficult to carry.

(iii) With period of time it looks very shabby.

(iv) No privacy for the guest checking in.

(v) If the book is misplaced all information is lost.

(2) Registration Card

This is a form of Registration record which usually has three copies, A leaf-top copy, record coloured copy, used as a C-form, and a hard copy. The flimsy copy (top one) is usually filled and kept for record whereas the hard copy is offered into the register before being filed. The registration of V.I.P.'s are normally pre-registered. It preserves privacy and serves as C-form, while easy to handover to the customer.

DEALING WITH GROUPS

A Group is a body of 15 or more. Because it involves volume business, special care has to be taken to ensure efficient handling of groups. Group travel is usually organised by travel agents, Tour operators or organisations planning convention, Seminars, conferences, etc. When handling group booking, first consider the type of group checking in. All details must be thoroughly discussed with the agent/group plans, baggage handlings, tipping, method of payment by group for extras should be clarified.

The group booking form must be completed by the organiser giving full details from which the hotel will be able to organise all the services required. There is usually a cancellation deadline on a group reservation after which the agent will be billed when finalising the agreements and confirming the reservations. It's better to include names of all members, rooming requirements, special requests, nationality and passport numbers.

Groups can register in any of the following three ways.

(i) Group can register in the usual way i.e. when they arrive each individual completes a separate registration form.

(ii) Individual registration forms could be dispensed with the list of names, initials, nationality and passport number to be handed in by Tour operator. This method is not exactly reliable as the information given may not be accurate.

(iii) Individual registration forms could be given to the tour operators for completion by guest en route to the hotel. It is then a simple matter of handling the registration form at reception on arrival. Arrival of group can cause lots of pressure on the reception and bell desk. Usually a group co-ordinator is assigned to look after the group arrivals, the luggage is tagged at the airport and on arrival the luggage goes directly to the respective guest rooms and keys are handed over to the guest leader along with a rooming list.

Usually group accounts and separate guest folios are opened where extras will be charged to the guest room number and settlement of this done before check out. A tour operator voucher will have to be sent to the hotel with confirmation and rooming list. On check-out the leader will hand over a copy of voucher signed by him detailing all charges for which the operator will be responsible.

The group departure, if not handled properly can cause chaos. All bills for extras, should be settled before baggages are removed and the keys are collected.

Arrival Notifications Slip

This notification slip is sent to various departments, at the time when the guest checks-in. This slip is sent to the following departments.

(a) General Manager.

(b) Front Office Manager.

(c) Bell Desk.

(d) Maintenance Department.

(e) Room Service.

(f) Telephones.

(g) Executive chef.

(h) House keeping.

(i) Cashier.

The notification slips are sent to the above mentioned departments, for the efficient functioning of the hotels. For example, when the telephone department receives the notification slip they connect the line (if it was disconnected when the room was vacant).

Also for example the executive chef should know about the occupancy of the hotel, so that accordingly he can prepare the indent. House keeping department should know about the occupancy to ensure efficient assignment of duties. Cashier will need it because he would be opening the guest folio. Similarly two other departments like—Bell desk and maintenance department receive the notification slips. These are also sent to the G.M. and F.O.M.

Arrival and Departure Register

This is used to maintain an account of the check-ins and check outs on a particular day. After the guest checks in, the register is updated. It is the duty of a front office assistant to keep the register updated. Formats of arrival and departure register, arrival notification slip, group booking form and message slip are given hereunder:

ARRIVAL AND DEPARTURE REGISTER

ARRIVAL NOTIFICATION SLIP

Message Slip

This plays a vital role in communication in a hotel, when an in-house guest is not present in the hotel and when a person wants to leave a message for a guest staying in the hotel.

The person who takes the message signs on it. There are two copies of message slip, original one is placed in the key rack, the duplicate one is sent to the room.

Key Card

Hotels give a Key Card to their guests, when they check in. The Key Card has the following details:

(i) Guest name

(ii) Room No.

(iii) Room Rate

(iv) Arrival Date

(v) Departure Date.

On the face of it inside, it gives the details of all other outlets at the hotel. The key card also acts as an identification for a guest. It can be used as a security check when the guests collect their keys.

It also brings to the attention of the guests the room rate when they register.

The key card is given to the guest by the receptionist and shows that the check in procedure is coming close to completion. I

Keys: The key itself may not be kept at reception since in the larger hotels it will almost certainly be held by the porters or at the information desk.

Keys are usually large to prevent clients from taking them away. The tag is usually marked with the room number and the I name of the hotel.

When the inhouse guest goes out of the hotel he gives the key to the information desk and when he returns after presenting the key card he gets it back.

No, Tariff	*For your convenience, please*	Our Facilities: RSi
carry this card with you for identification. You are	6.30 AM to 11.00 PM	
required to produce this card	KYB Restaurant 11.	
when requesting for your key,		
signing in the Restaurants and	7.00PM to 11.00PM	
Bars and on final check out.		
Room Key	The hotel will not be	French Connection Bar
Card	responsible for any loss of	11.00 AM to 11.00PM
money or valuables left in the	Buffet Breakfast	
room. Safe Deposit Boxes are	07.00 AM to 10.30 AM	
available at the Cashier's		
Counter.		
We wish you a pleasant stay at	Room Service Bills are	
(Hotel's Name)	debited to your room bill.	
Do not therefore pay cash		
to room boys.		

FRONT OFFICE MANAGEMENT COMPONENTS

(a) Front Desk Representative

The first contact many guests have with your property is with your front desk employees. Make the most of that contact by fully preparing your front desk staff for everything from check-in fo check-out. They will learn: how to use all front desk equipment, including the computer, printer, and telephone; every step of check-in procedures—from preparation to follow-up; how to service guests during their stay; proper check-out procedures that leave a lasting, favourable impression; employees who complete this guide are ready to pursue Hospitality Skills Certification.

(b) Bell Attendant

Bell attendants provide more than luggage service to guests—they are a measure of your property's ability to provide outstanding service in all areas. Make sure they are well-equipped to deliver. With this guide, they will learn: qualities necessary to be an outstanding bell attendant; how to handle security issues such as key control; how to deal with guests under the influence of alcohol.

(c) PBX Operator

Your PBX operators are the voice of your property. Is it an enthusiastic, friendly, efficient voice or one your guests are glad to hang up on? This comprehensive guide gives PBX operators the skills to: proficiently use the phone system for everything from placing international calls to making wake-up calls; respond to emergencies such as fire alarms, bomb threats, and inclement weather; follow all appropriate guest privacy and security measures.

(d) Concierge

It is been described as the most difficult job at a full service property—but it just got easier. This comprehensive guide provides a framework of knowledge and skill expectations for one of the most visible positions at a property. It covers: qualities needed to make a good concierge; and how to handle typical and unusual guest requests.

(e) Reservationist

Reservationists can make the difference between a profitable occupancy rate and a bleak one. This guide gives them all the skills they need to be powerful sales tools for your property. Reservationists will learn to use effective telephone sales techniques, accurately take and process reservations, and prepare room availability forecasts.

(f) Retail Cashier

Retail operations, from gift shops to specialty kiosks, are becoming important profit centres for lodging properties. Make sure that the retail cashiers who staff these facilities have the same hospitality skills as the rest of your staff, so that guests have a consistent service experience. This guide provides step-by-step task breakdowns and job knowledge for retail cashiers, including information on telephone courtesy, retail sales skills, point-of-sale equipment, and retail operations and the lodging property environment.

(g) Valet Attendant

Your guests' interaction with the valet attendant may provide the first impression they have of your property. Ensure that the impression is a great one, by providing your valet attendants with the job knowledge and task information they need to perform to the highest service standards. This guide includes step-by-step training information on a variety of valet skills, including the telephone system, handling luxury limousines, respecting guests' vehicles and property, and reporting tips.

COMMUNICATION WITHIN FRONT OFFICE

LOG BOOK

- The front office generally maintains a log book, which is an important format which makes the front office staff aware of important events and decisions that occurred during previous workshifts.
- A typical front office log book is a daily journal, which chronicles unusual events, guest complaints or requests, and other relevant information.
- The front desk agents record in the log book throughout their shift. These notes should be clearly written in a prescribed form so that they serve as effective reference material for the next shift.
- Before the beginning of the shift, front desk supervisors and agents should review and initial log book, noting any current activities, situations that require follow-up or potential problems.
- The front office is important for the management as it helps the management to understand the activity of the front desk and it records any ongoing issues.

INFORMATION DIRECTORY

- The front office staff must be able to respond in a knowledgeable way when guests contact the front desk for information.
- Some front offices accumulate such data in a bound guide called an information directory.
- The following are the main information provided by the information directory: -
    - Local restaurant recommendations.
    - Contacting a taxi company.
    - Directions to the local companies.

- o Directions to the nearest shopping center, drug store, etc.
- o Directions to the nearest places of worship.
- o Directions to the nearest bank or the automated teller machine.
- o Direction to the theater, stadium, or ticket agency.
- o Directions to the universities, libraries, museums, or other points of local interest.
- o Directions to the local courts or the city hall.
- o Information about the hotel policies.
- o Information about the hotel's recreational facilities or those near the hotel.
- Some hotels have installed computer information terminals in public areas including the lobby area.
- These terminals are essentially an electronic equivalent of the front office information directory.
- Guests without front office assistance easily access computer-based information terminals.
- In addition, many hotels provide a printed schedule of daily events or display a daily event board through a closed-circuit television system.
- A common industry term for displaying daily events is the reader board. Printed itineraries may be place at the front desk, in elevators, and throughout the lobby area.

MAIL AND PACKAGING HANDLING

- Registered guests rely on the front office to relay delivered mail and packages quickly and efficiently.
- Front office managers normally develop policies for mail and package handling based on the policies and regulations of the Indian Postal Department.
- In general, the front office is expected to time-stamp all guest mail when it arrives at the property. This answers any question arising regarding when the mail arrive at the property or how quickly the guest was noticed about its arrival.
- When the mail and packages arrives, the front office record should be checked to verify that the guest is about to arrive, is currently registered in the hotel or has departed from the hotel.

The front office should promptly notify the guest that a mail has been received from his behalf. Some properties notify

the guests by switching on an in-room message light on the guestroom telephone; others deliver a printed form to the telephone.
- Mail for guests who have not yet arrived: -
    1. If a mail arrives for a guest who has not yet registered, a notation should be made on the guest's reservation record.
    2. The mail safely kept in a drawer until the guest arrives.
- Mail for guests whop has already checked-out: -
    1. Guest mail that is not picked up or has arrived for a guest who has already checked out should be time stamped a second time and returned to its sender or sent to a forwarding address if the guest has provided one.

HANDLING OF REGISTERED MAIL

- Guests may also receive registered letters, express mail packages, or other mail requiring a signature on delivery.
- Some hotels permit the front desk agent to sign for such mail.
- Then, the agent records the item's delivery in the front office mail signature book, and has the guest sign for the mail in the book at the time of pick-up or delivery.

HANDLING OF PACKAGES

- Packages are usually handled as mail. If the package is too large to store at the front desk, it should be taken to a secure room.
- The package and its location should be recorded in the front office mail signature book.
- When mail or packages are received, it is customary to notify the guest immediately.

GUEST SERVICES

- As the center of front office activity, the front desk is responsible for co-coordinating the guest services.
- Typical guest services involve providing information and special equipments and supplies.
- Guest services may also include accommodating guests through special procedures.
- A request that is beyond the responsibility of the front office should be directly referred to the appropriate department.

🔖🔖 A growing number of hotels employ a concierge or other designated staff member to handle guest requests.

EQUIPMENT AND SUPPLIES

- Guests may request special equipment and supplies while making a reservation, at the time of registration, or during occupancy.
- Reservation agents should have a reliable method of recording the special requests to ensure that they are properly met.
- After registration, a guest who needs special equipment or supplies will almost always contact a front desk agent.
- Equipment and supplies commonly requested by the guests include: -

  a) Roll-away beds and cribs

  b) Additional linens / pillows

  c) Irons and ironing boards

  d) Additional cloth hangers

  e) Audiovisual and office equipment

  f) Special equipment for visually impaired, or physically challenged guests.
- The front desk agents should have alternative ways to meet guest requests when the department that normally provides the equipment or services is closed or inaccessible.
- In many hotels the front desk agent have the accessibility to the linen and housekeeping supplies room to provide the guests with the equipments required by them in the absence of any housekeeping staff.

SPECIAL PROCEDURES

- The guests may ask for special treatment when making a reservation, during registration, at the time of check-out or during occupancy.
- The reservation agents should have a reliable method of recording special requests made during the process of reservation and communicating such requests to appropriate front office staff.
- The front office staff should be empowered to handle the request and satisfy the guest if at all possible.

- Procedural requests may require more time and effort to fulfill than equipment and supply requests. Typical procedural request include: -

    a) **Split account folios : -**

This is generally requested by the business travelers to separate the room charges and taxes from the other charges such as food and beverage charges because some companies pay only the accommodation charges of their employees.

    b) **Master account folios : -**

This is generally requested by a convention group meeting to post only the authorized charges incurred in the hotel in to the master folio.

    c) **Wake-up calls : -**

The wake-up calls are requested by the guest requiring to perform some important tasks such as catching a flight early in the morning.

    d) **Transportation arrangements : -**

The guests may also require various transportation services from the hotel during arrival, occupancy or during their departure.

    e) **Newspaper delivery and secretarial services : -**

- A concierge may handle other procedural requests. Hotels not employing a concierge have a front desk agent to handle these requests.
- Some hotels operate a guest service center to handle the various special and procedural requests of the guests.

GUEST RELATIONS AND COMPLAINT HANDLING

GUEST RELATION

- The front office should develop strategies and tactics in anticipation of complaints made by the guest to resolve the situation and satisfy the guest.
- The high visibility of the front office means that front desk agents are the first to learn about the guest complaints.
- The front desk agent should always attentively listen to complaints made by the guest and seek a timely resolution to the problem.
- Employees should also realize that the guests who do not have the opportunity to complain often tell their friends, relatives and business associate about this.

✒ ✒ When the guests find it easy to express their opinions, both the hotel and the guest benefit. The hotel learns of potential or actual problems and has the opportunity to resolve them thus satisfying the guest.

✒ ✒ When the problems are easily resolved, the guest thinks that the hotel cares about his needs.

COMPLAINTS HANDLING

✒ ✒ There are four categories of problems associated complaints: -

a) Mechanical Complaints: -

✒ ✒ Most guest complaints relate to the malfunction of the hotel equipments.

✒ ✒ This generally include problems with climate control, lighting, electricity, room furnishings, ice machines, vending machines, door keys, plumbing, television sets, elevators and so on.

✒ ✒ Effective use of the log book and maintenance work orders may reduce the frequency of the mechanical complaints.

✒ ✒ It is therefore required that appropriate staff member should be should be dispatched as quickly as possible with the proper tools to fix the problem.

b) Attitudinal Complaints: -

✒ ✒ The guests may make attitudinal complaints when they feel insulted by rude behavior of the staffs.

✒ ✒ Guests who overhear staff conversations or who complaints from the hotel staff members may also express attitudinal complaints.

✒ ✒ Managers and supervisors should listen and attend to the complaints and problems of staff. This can be especially critical to maintain solid guest relations.

c) Service-related Complaints: -

✒ ✒ Guests make service-related complaints when they experience a problem with hotel service.

✒ ✒ Service –related complaints may be wide-ranging and may include long waiting time for service, lack of assistance with luggage, untidy rooms, phone difficulties, missed wake-up calls, cold or ill-prepared food, or ignored request for additional supplies.

d) Unusual Complaints: -

- Guests may also complaint about the absence of swimming pool, lack of transportation services and bad weather and so on.
- Hotels have little or no control over the situations involving unusual complaints.
- The front office management should therefore alert front desk agents that on occasion guest may complain about the things a staff can do nothing.
- Through such orientation, staff will be better prepared to handle an unusual situation with appropriate guest relations techniques and avoid a potentially difficult encounter.
- **The following are the guidelines, a front office management and staff should keep while handling the guest complaints: -**
- When expressing a complaint, the guest may be quite angry. Front office staff members should not go alone to a guestroom to investigate a problem or otherwise risk potential danger.
- Front office staff members should not make promises that exceed their authority.
- If a problem cannot be solved, front office staff should admit this to the guest early on. Honesty is the best policy when dealing with guest complaints.
- Front desk agents should be advised that some guests complain as part of their nature, the front office should develop an approach for dealing with such guests.

FOLLOW-UP PROCEDURES

- Front office management may use the front office log book to initiate corrective action, verify that the guest complaints have been resolved, and identify recurring problems.
- This written record may also enable management to contact guests who may still be dissatisfied with some aspect of their stay at check-out.
- After the guest has departed, a letter from the front office manager expressing regret about the about the incident can promote the goodwill of the hotel.
- It may be step from the part of the front office manager to telephone a departed guest to get a more complete description of the incident.

- ✦ ✦ Chain hotels may also receive guest complaints channeled through chain headquarters.
- ✦ ✦ Records of guest complaints about eh hotels in the chain may be compiled and sent to each manager.
- ✦ ✦ This method of feedback allows the chin's corporate headquarters to evaluate and compare each hotel's guest relations performance.

HANDLING COMPLAINTS

HOUSEKEEPING

- The housekeeping department and the front office must keep each other informed of changes in room status to ensure that guests are roomed efficiently and without complication.
- The more familiar front office staffs are with housekeeping procedures, and vice versa, the sooner the relationship will be between the two departments.

ENGINERRING AND MAINTENANCE

- In many hotels, engineering and maintenance personnel begin each shift by examining the front office log book for repair work orders.
- Front desk agents use the log book to track maintenance problems reported by guests or staff, such as poor heating or cooling, faulty plumbing, noisy equipment, or broken furniture.
- The front office log book serves as an excellent reference for hotel's engineering and maintenance staff.
- If a maintenance problem renders a room unsalable, housekeeping must be informed immediately when the problem is resolved so the room can be placed back in the available room inventory.

DURING THE STAY ACTIVITIES

INFORMATION SERVICES

THE INFORMATION DESK

- The Information Desk of the front office is also an important section of the department and plays an important role in give the guests and visitors valuable information about the hotel and the city at large.
- The information desk is operated by a Concierge who is also known as the information assistant.

- The concierge provides important information to the guests and the visitors about the various facilities and services of the hotel and also gives important information about the city such as the routes to the nearest airport or railway station or hospitals and banks.
- The concierge also plays an important in arranging tickets for the guests in various concerts taking place in the city.

INFORMATION DIRECTORY

- The front office staff must be able to respond in a knowledgeable way when guests contact the front desk for information.
- Some front offices accumulate such data in a bound guide called an information directory.
- The following are the main information provided by the information directory: -
    - Local restaurant recommendations.
    - Contacting a taxi company.
    - Directions to the local companies.
    - Directions to the nearest shopping center, drug store, etc.
    - Directions to the nearest places of worship.
    - Directions to the nearest bank or the automated teller machine.
    - Direction to the theater, stadium, or ticket agency.
    - Directions to the universities, libraries, museums, or other points of local interest.
    - Directions to the local courts or the city hall.
    - Information about the hotel policies.
    - Information about the hotel's recreational facilities or those near the hotel.

READERS BOARD

- The Reader's Board is a very important tool of providing information to the guests, visitors and patrons of the hotel.
- The Reader's Board is located in the lobby of the hotel and consists of a velvet board with a golden metallic boarder and the board is fixed with the help of a stand.
- The board shows all the current events which are presently taking place in the hotel such as wedding ceremonies in the banquets, meetings, conferences and other important official events, festivals and exhibitions taking place in the hotel.

- The events are shown on the board with golden alphabets on a red velvet background and thus, are clearly visible to the guests, patrons and visitors to the hotel.

TENT CARD

- The tent card is also a very important tool of promoting the hotel to the in-house guests of the hotel and displays important features and events of the hotel.
- The tent card is a card made of glossy paper and looks like a tent and is kept on the reading table of the guest in the guestroom.
- The card elicits important information about the hotel to the in-house regarding the facilities and services of the hotel and the events taking place in the property.

MESSAGES AND MAIL HANDLING

HANDLING INCOMING MESSAGES OF GUESTS (VERBAL AS WELL AS TELEPHONE)

- Inform the guest about the caller and transfer the call to the guest on request according to the instructions of the guest
- Call the guest to make sure that he or she is present in the guestroom
- Press the message light outside the guestroom for the guest to know about the message

  1st **copy** of slip in the key and message hole

  2nd **copy** of slip inside the guestroom

  3rd **copy** of slip in front desk for records

- Note down the message in a triplicate copy of message book
- Guest may be in room
- Guest not in room
- Mark the reservation file or envelope of the guest and record the message in the log of the reception
- If the reservation of the guest exists, then take the message for the guest on the slip
- Check whether the reservation of the guest exists in the hotel
- Guest is staying in the hotel

- Guest is not staying in the hotel
- Check if the guest is staying in the hotel

HANDLING OF MAILS AT THE INFORMATION COUNTER OF FRONT OFFICE

- Mail either kept at the key and mail hole of the front desk or with the lobby manager in absence of the guest and then delivered to the guest
- Mail kept at a separate drawer and the reservation slip is marked with "letter"
- Mail redirected to the address of the check-out guest
- Check the name of the in-house guest against information rack
- Check the name of the guest against the reservation rack
- Check the address of the check-out guest against mail forwarding cards
- Mail of Guest who are yet to arrive
- Mail of In-house guest
- Mail of Check-out guest
- Employee Mail
- Mail of general manager sent to his office
- Department mail sent to respective departments
- Place the mails of the guests in an alphabetical rack
- Hotel Mail
- Employee Mail
- Sorting of the guest mail alphabetically after time stamping them

GUESTROOM KEY CONTROL

- One of reception's important jobs have been issuing room keys to the guests and them take them back for safe keeping when the guests went out.
- The keys had a large and heavy tags attached to them to stop gusts from walking off with them.
- The tags were numbered so that the keys could be hung on a *"key rack"* when not in use. The key rack was usually situated behind the desk.

- The old fashioned metal key was a security risk. Guests often missed or mislaid them.
- Thus the modern hotels started using electronic keys as a solution to the problem. These keys were made of plastic and punched or magnetically coded with the door code.
- These keys do not have the room number printed on them, so the guest has to be given an additional key card showing this.
- So, the guest has to keep this card separate from the electronic room key in case the latter is stolen.
- The room lock is programmed to accept only the code on the electronic key, which is changed every time the room is let.

Electronic Key Card System:

- An electronic locking system replaces traditional mechanical locks with sophisticated computer-based guestroom access devices.
- A centralized locking system operates through a master control console at the front desk which is wired to every guestroom door.
- At registration, a front desk agent inserts a key or card in to the appropriate room slot at the front desk console to transmit its code to the guestroom door lock.
- These locks can be designed to use a magnetic key card or a special high-security card.

Advantages of the Electronic Keys:

- These electronic keys are relatively cheaper than the metal keys, so their loss does not matter much.
- These electronic keys have cut down the number of thefts from rooms by a significant amount.
- They have eliminated the time wasting process of taking keys in and handling them out.
- Thus they allow the receptionist to concentrate on productive contacts with guests.

HOSPITALITY DESK

DEFINITION

The Hospitality Desk is a part of the front office department which deals in all such services that are offered to the guest either complimentary or are available at very little charge.

STAFF

The Hospitality Desk is generally managed by the Guest Relation Executive, hostesses and airport executives.

SERVICES PROVIDED BY THE HOSPITALITY DESK

1. *Aarti, Tika* and Garlanding of VVIP, VIP and foreigner guests
2. Personalized stationery
3. Flowers and fruits in the guestroom
4. Free airport pick-up and drop to the VVIP and VIP guests
5. Assistance in shopping
6. Guiding foreign guest on tours and shopping
7. Baby-sitting

FUNCTIONS OF THE HOSPITALITY DESK

1. Welcoming the VIP guests on arrival
2. Courtesy call to VIP guests
3. Ensuring comfortable stay for the VIP guests
4. Escorting the VIP guests to the rooms

COMPLAINTS HANDLING

TYPES OF COMPLAINTS

a) MECHANICAL COMPLAINTS: -

- Most guest complaints relate to the malfunction of the hotel equipments.
- This generally include problems with climate control, lighting, electricity, room furnishings, ice machines, vending machines, door keys, plumbing, television sets, elevators and so on.

b) ATTITUDINAL COMPLAINTS: -

- The guests may make attitudinal complaints when they feel insulted by rude behavior of the staffs.
- Guests who overhear staff conversations or who complaints from the hotel staff members may also express attitudinal complaints.

c) SERVICE-RELATED COMPLAINTS: -

- Guests make service-related complaints when they experience a problem with hotel service.
- Service –related complaints may be wide-ranging and may include long waiting time for service, lack of assistance with luggage, untidy rooms, phone difficulties, missed wake-up calls, cold or ill-prepared food, or ignored request for additional supplies.

d) UNUSUAL COMPLAINTS: -

- Guests may also complaint about the absence of swimming pool, lack of transportation services and bad weather and so on.
- Hotels have little or no control over the situations involving unusual complaints.

GUIDELINS FOR COMPLAINT HANDLING

- When expressing a complaint, the guest may be quite angry. Front office staff members should not go alone to a guestroom to investigate a problem or otherwise risk potential danger.
- Front office staff members should not make promises that exceed their authority.
- If a problem cannot be solved, front office staff should admit this to the guest early on. Honesty is the best policy when dealing with guest complaints.
- Front desk agents should be advised that some guests complain as part of their nature, the front office should develop an approach for dealing with such guests.

STEPS TO FOLLOWED IN HANDLING COMPLAINTS

1. AVOID CONFLICT
2. LISTEN TO THE GUEST PATIENTLY
3. SHOW SYMPATHY TOWARDS THE GUEST AND APOLOGIZE FOR THE POOR SERVICE
4. DO NOT JUSTIFY UNTILL AND UNLESS THE SITUATION DEMANDS
5. ASK QUESTIONS TO LEARN ABOUT THE DETAILS OF THE COMPLAINT
6. TAKE ACTION

7. FOLLOW UP WITH THE GUEST AFTER THE ACTION HAS BEEN TAKEN
8. TAKE FEEDBACK FROM THE GUEST

GUEST HSITORY

GUEST HISTORY CARD

- Guest History Management is a very important function of the front office department of the hotel.
- Most of the front office departments of hotels maintain records of the guests coming to the hotel which helps them to create a database of the guests and take care of the special considerations of the guests whenever they arrive the next time at the hotel.
- These records of the financial and personal information of the guests are maintained in formats which are called Guest History Cards.
- The guest history cards serve as important tools of information for the front office management and help the front office to draft a profile of the guest based on his or her previous stay.
- The information in the guest history card is taken by the front office assistant at the time of reservation, registration and also at the time of the departure of the guests from the hotel.
- Thus, guest history management helps the hotel to maintain a good relationship with the guests and also helps the hotel management to get rid of unwanted guests by refusing them guestrooms.

NAME: NATIONALITY:

ADDRESS: DATE OF BIRTH:

WEDDING ANNIVERSARY:

ANY OTHER IMPORTANT DATES:

ARRIVAL DATE NO. OF DAYS ROOM NO. PREFERENCE IF ANY NORMALLY BOOKED THROUGH

AGENT / CO.

CONTACT

NORMAL BILLING

INSTRUCTIONS

COMMENTS IF ANY:

NIGHT AUDIT IN FRONT OFFICE

SOME IMPORTANT TERMS USED IN THE NIGHT AUDIT ROUTINE

1. Audit Trail : An organized flow of source documents detailing each step in the processing of a transaction.

2. Daily Transcript : A detailed report of all guests accounts that indicates each charge transaction affecting a guest account for the day, used as a worksheet to detect posting errors.

3. Supplemental Transcript : A detailed report of all non-guest accounts that indicates each charge transaction that affected a non-guest account that day, used as a worksheet to detect posting errors.

4. End-of-day : An arbitrary stopping point for the business day.

5. Room Status Report : A report that allows the front desk agent to identify the ready rooms, typically prepared as a part of the night audit.

6. Room Variance Report : A report listing any discrepancies between front desk and housekeeping room statuses.

7. System Update : A fully automated audit routine accomplishing the same functions as a non-computerised night audit; daily system updates enable file reorganization, system maintenance, and report production, and provide an end-of-day time frame.

8. Bucket Check : The night auditor's check of room rate postings on guest folios against the housekeeping department's report of occupied rooms and the front desk room rack; helps ensure that rates have been posted for all occupied rooms and helps reduce the occupancy errors caused when front desk agents do not properly complete check-in and check-out procedures.

9. In Balance : A term used to describe the state of accounts when the totals of debit amounts and credit amounts are equal.

10. Out-of-balance : A term used to describe the state of accounts when the total of debit amounts and credit amounts are not equal.

11. Control Folio : An accounting department document used internally by a front office computer to support all account postings by department during a system update routine.

12. D card : A night auditor's report used in semi-automated front office accounting systems.

THE NIGHT AUDIT AND ITS MAIN FUNCTIONS

FUNCTIONS OF NIGHT AUDIT

- The front office must regularly review and verify the accuracy and completeness of the guest and the non-guest accounting records.
- The front office audit is a daily review of guest account transactions recorded at the front desk against revenue centre transactions.
- The routine front office audit helps to guarantee the accuracy, reliability, and the thoroughness of front office accounting.
- The front office audit is usually called the night audit because hotels generally perform the same during the late evening hours.

THE MAIN FUNCTIONS OF THE NIGHT AUDIT

- Verification of the posted entries to the guest and non-guest accounts.
- Balancing all the front office accounts.
- Resolution of the room status discrepancies.
- Monitoring the guest credit limits.
- Production of the various operational and managerial reports.

THE ROLE OF THE NIGHT AUDITOR

- The night auditor should be familiar with the nature of the cash transactions affecting the front office accounting system.
- The night auditor typically tracks the room revenues, occupancy percentage, and other standard operating statistics.
- In addition, the auditor prepares a daily summary of the cash, check, and credit card activities that occurred at the front desk.
- The night auditor summarizes and reports the results of operations to front office management.

DETAILS OF THE NIGHT AUDIT PROCESS

THE TIME OF THE NIGHT AUDIT

- The night auditor generally works in the night shift, from 2300 Hrs. to 0700 Hrs.
- The business day of a hotel ends with the beginning of the night audit process.

- The period in between the audit when the same is taking place is called the **Audit Work Time**.
- Generally the night audit starts at around 0100 Hrs. in most of the hotel except the casino hotels where the night audit takes place at around 0400 Hrs.

THE AUDIT POSTING FORMULA USED IN THE FRONT OFFICE

Previous Balance + Debits - Credits = Net Outstanding Balance

PB DR CR NOB

THE TEN STEPS OF NIGHT AUDIT

The following are the ten steps of the night audit process in front office:

1. Completion of Outstanding Postings.
2. Reconciliation of Room Status Discrepancies.
3. Balancing All Departmental Accounts.
4. Verification of the Room Rates
5. Verification of the No-show reservations.
6. Posting Room Rates and Taxes.
7. Preparation of Required Reports.
8. Preparation of Cash Receipts for Deposit.
9. Clear or Back Up the System.
10. Distribution of the Reports.

BRIEF DESCRIPTION OF THE TEN STEPS OF THE NIGHT AUDIT PROCESS

1. Completion of Outstanding Postings:-

- One of the primary functions of the night audit is to ensure that all transactions affecting guest and non-guest accounts are posted to appropriate folios before the end of the day.
- Traditionally, the first step of the night audit is to complete all outstanding postings.
- The night auditor should therefore confirm that all transactions have been posted to the proper accounts as they are received at the front desk before starting the audit routine.
- In addition to completing the posting function, the auditor verifies that all vouchers for revenue centre transactions are posted.

- In an automated hotel, this is done by generating printed posting reports from the accounting system.
- If the figures are identical, the systems are in balance. If they are not the same, the auditor begins to compare transactions that have been omitted or improperly posted.

2. Reconciliation of Room Status Discrepancies:-
- Room status discrepancies should be resolved in time during the night audit process since imbalances can lead to lost business and thus cause confusion in the front office.
- Errors in room status can lead to lost and uncollectible room revenue and omissions in postings.
- The front office should maintain accurate room status information to effectively determine the number and types of rooms available for sale.
- At the end of the day, the room status report is compared with the housekeeper's report and the bucket where the registration cards for in-house guests are kept.
- In automated hotels, the checkout process is normally linked to a room management function that automatically monitors and updates the room status.
- Though the room status discrepancies are rare in automated hotels, the night audit process is still necessary to ensure accuracy.

3. Balancing All Departmental Accounts:-
- It is generally considered more easy for the front office staffs to balance all the departments first and then look for posting errors with-in an out-of-balance department in order to avoid discovering errors in the night audit process.
- The night auditor typically balances all the revenue centre departments using the source documents that originated in the revenue centre.
- The night auditor balances all front office transactions against the departmental transaction information.
- The process used to balance the revenue centre departments is often called the trial balance.
- The trial balance usually uncovers any corrections or adjustments that need to be made during the night audit process.

- The trial balance is performed before posting the room rates and thus, if the trial balance is correct but the final balance is wrong, then the auditor can find that the error has been made in the posting of the room rates and taxes.
- Thus, performing the trial balance before the room rates posting avoids the creation of confusion during the night audit process due to the errors.

4. Verification of Room Rates:-

- The night auditor has to verify the room rates properly before posting them in the guest accounts.
- The night auditor has to check that proper rates have been allotted to the guest on the basis of the plans, package, discounts etc.
- The proper use of room revenue and count information can form a solid basis for room revenue analysis.
- The night auditor is responsible for calculating the room revenue and reporting it as part of the night audit or it may be done automatically by the front office computer system.

5. Verifying the No-show Reservations:-

- The night auditor is responsible for clearing the reservation rack and post charges to no-show accounts.
- While posting the no-show charges, the night audit should carefully verify that the reservation was guaranteed and the guest did not register in the hotel.
- The no-show billing should be handled with great care by correctly recording the transactions.
- The night auditor should properly bill the no-show guests since incorrect billing may lead the credit card company to revaluate its legal agreement and relationship with the hotel.
- All front office staff must adhere to established no-show procedures when handling reservation cancellation or modifications.

6. Posting of Room Rates and Taxes

- The posting of room rates and taxes takes place at the end of the business day.
- Once the room rates are posted, a room rate and tax report is generated for the front office management review.

- In the automated hotels, the room rates and taxes are posted in the individual guest folios automatically at one go.
- Once the night auditor verifies the room rates and the taxes to posted, the computer automatically posts the room rates and taxes in the individual guest folios in few minutes.
- In addition, the automatic charge postings are accurate, with no chance for pick-up, tax calculation or posting errors.
- Thus, the auto-posting of room rates and taxes can save night audit time and improve accuracy in night audit.

7. Preparation of Reports:-

- The night auditor prepares reports that indicate the status of front office activities and operations.
- The following are the important reports generated by the night auditor during the night audit:

Daily Operations Report

- The daily operations report summarizes the day's business and provides insight into revenues, operating statistics, and cash transactions related to the front office.
- This report is considered the most important outcome of the front office audit.

High Balance Report

- The high balance report identifies guests whose charges are approaching an account credit limit designated by the hotel.
- In automated hotels, the high balance report may be produced at any time during the day.

Group Summary Report

- The group summary report generally details the various activities of the groups registered in the hotel.
- It generally shows the number of rooms occupied by each group in the hotel, the number of guests for each group, and the revenue generated by each group.

VIPs Report

- The VIPs report gives information about the total number of VIP guests registered in the hotel.

- This report is useful for providing various special services to these guests and also for the hotel in its ability to draw such type of elite guests.

8. Deposition Of Cash:-

- The night auditor prepares a cash deposit voucher as an important part of the night audit process.
- If the front office cash receipts have not been deposited in the bank, the auditor compares the postings of cash payments and paid-outs with actual cash on hand.
- A copy of the front office cashier shift report may be included in the cash deposit envelope to support any overage, shortage, or due back balances.
- Since account and departmental balancing often involve cash transactions, accurate cash depositing may depend on an effective audit process.

9. Clear or Back Up the system:-

- In manual and semi-automated system of front office operations, the totals must be cleared from the system after the night audit is complete.
- Manual systems are cleared by moving the closing balance from the night audit report to the opening balance of the next day's report.
- In semi-automated systems, the totals in the account posting machine must be brought to zero balance.
- A system back-up in the night audit routine is unique to the computerised front office systems.
- Computer generated front office information should be copied onto magnetic disk depending the system configuration.
- Many computer systems have two types of system back-up.
  - *A daily back-up* simply creates a copy of the front office electronic files on magnetic disk or tape.
  - *A weekly back-up* which not only copies the daily information, but also eliminates account transactions information which are of no value any more.

10. Distribution of Reports:-

- It is an essential responsibility of the night auditor to properly hand over the various reports of the night audit to the authorized and designated individuals due to the confidential nature of the reports.
- The distribution of the reports prepared is the final step of the night audit routine.
- Managerial decisions can be properly made only if the reports are properly, accurately and timely completed.

THE VARIOUS TYPES OF ERRORS IN THE NIGHT AUDIT

- Numerous types of errors occurred in the various transactions of the front office can be easily identified during the night audit process.
- These errors mostly occur due to faulty posting and clerical operation.
- The following are some of the common errors made in the front office:

♦ Pickup Errors:

- This type of error is common in the manual and the semi-automated front office systems.
- This type of error occurs when a previous closing balance of a particular day have been wrongly written as the opening balance of the next day.
- Thus the resulting closing balance of the following day will also become incorrect.
- Thus, the front office cashier should properly access the previous balance of an account folio, post the debits and credits, and calculate a new current balance.

♦ Transposition Errors:

- This type of error is also common in the manual and the semi-automated front office systems.
- This type of error occurs when numbers related to a transaction are reversed. **(For instance, writing or entering $523 instead of $532 in the account posting machine.)**

- A transposition error can usually be identified by subtracting the smaller number from the larger number and dividing the result by 9. If the result is a whole number, then the problem is mostly likely to be a transposition error.

♦ **Missing Folios:**
  - This type of error is also common in the semi and non-automated front office systems.
  - Due to the incorrect filing of the folios or removal of the same from the folio bucket, often the front office systems become out of balance.
  - This normally occurs when the front office cashier forgetfully allows the guest folio to remain behind the room tab instead of bringing the same to the front of the room tab after the departure of the guest.
  - Folios can also seem to misplace if the front office cashier of a particular shift forgets to inform the front office cashier of the next shift that the same has been sent to the credit manager for his review.
  - Thus, the front office cashier should handle the guest folios with great care to avoid the inconvenience caused by missing the same.

Yield and Revenue Management Systems: Applications and Future Prospects

YIELD MANAGEMENT SYSTEM MEASUREMENT

When a hotel with an installed yield management system experiences in its first year a healthy growth in revenues from bookings, compared to the previous year when it did not use a system, who or what should get credit for the improved revenue performance? An argument can be made that the system really delivered benefits. However, the Sales and Marketing Department can claim that the new advertising campaigns and direct mail brought in greater volume. The Guest Services Department may claim higher guest satisfaction ratings generated considerable repeat business. The hotel's management team may point to the fact that the property was operating in a much improved local economic environment. Considering all of these factors—and the activities enacted to affect revenue performance—one could even ask whether or not the yield management system is actually delivering benefits. Consequently, measuring the impact of the yield management system is essential to correctly attribute what revenue increases are a result of the system or are a result of other factors. Plus, true system measurement is required for hotel owners and executives, who need to justify the purchase of the system, precisely understand return on investment, and prove system impact for a rollout. In the hospitality industry, there have been many approaches and technologies offered to provide yield management benefits. Likewise, there have been many attempts to help hoteliers see and understand what their yield management systems are doing for them. Successful measurement can only occur when the hotel measures its performance working with the yield management system, and compare it to the revenue performance it would" have received without the system, everything else being equal. Let's take a look at five of the more well-known measurement approaches.

A. Historical Revenues Trends Analysis

The hotelier plots daily revenues from the past several years, and searches his or her findings for any type of trends. Spikes from the statistical noise produced from seasonality and demand fluctuations are smoothed to determine stable patterns. The patterns are used as a basis for making future projections, which are expected to grow at a steady rate. By comparing the future projections with any deviation from the projections, the amount of deviation, in theory, may be tied to the system. However, this approach fails to account for the impact of new events that happened after the system was installed—new marketing campaigns or the introduction of a web site, for example, which were not done in the past. It still makes it impossible to see what revenue change is due to the system or to other factors.

B. "After the Fact" Review

A process is used to estimate what the unconstrained demand would have been or may have been. The process considers demand "on the books" and, after there is no more hotel capacity, it attempts to figure the amount of demand turned down. With this information in hand, the hotelier speculates that, if he or she accepted the best business mix after the fact, how much revenue would have the property generated. That amount is compared to the actual amount of revenues. This difference or "gap" offers a possible measure for improvement. The "gap" before the system install is weighed against the "gap" after the system installation. The difference perhaps illustrates the system's impact. Simply, this approach only teaches the hotelier how to be wiser after the event, instead of making the best decisions for future booking opportunities. If you made investment decisions, in the stock market, for example, solely after the fact, knowing how prices fluctuated, and realizing when would have been the best time to buy and sell, you still would not enjoy optimum return because the decisions did not factor future volatility and uncertainty. This approach cannot separate what the system is doing and what is being affected by changing market conditions and other factors.

C. Comparison of Hotels within Competitive Set

In an attempt to estimate the yield management system results, revenues from a period after system installation are compared to a similar period last year prior to installation. To consider the effect of extraneous factors on revenues, the comparison is tracked against any demand fluctuations from a similar hotel (without the yield management system) in the same competitive set, and/or with nearly the same demographics.

Hotels and resorts pride themselves in their uniqueness. So it is impossible to imagine two hotels that would experience identical affects from the extraneous factors, and it is highly unlikely they would share the same pricing strategies directed or the same marketing mixes.

D. Computer Simulation in Controlled Environments

It is vital that the system measurement is conducted in such a manner as to isolate the changes in market conditions and the business environment. One of the first places where this type of system measurement with isolation was attempted was in a controlled environment, using computer simulation. In this case, a yield management practice with basic demand data is deployed. First, booking decisions from the yield management practice are based on simulated human decisions, which result in bookings accepted and not accepted. Next, the booking decisions are based on yield management system decisions. Again, bookings are accepted and not accepted. Accepted bookings from both decision scenarios translate into revenue, and the compared revenues between the two illustrate how the yield management practice may deliver results. However, how can computer simulation understand truly how the humans would have acted? Humans are not efficient at executing on "first come and first served." Even if the measurement shows benefits in a controlled environment, how can the hotelier be assured that there will be benefits in the "real" world. It is impossible to predict in a controlled setting how the users would interact with the system.

E. True Scientific Measurement

If demand does increase due to marketing programmes or an improvement in economy after the yield system installation, occupancy will increase, and there will be more sold-out nights. But what if there is no increase in demand compared to last year, while an effective yield management practice is put into place? As a result of the yield management system, it is anticipated that there will be a reduction in the number of turn downs multi-night stays. And the proper overbooking of rooms leads to a decrease in the amount of empty rooms on sold-out nights. Thus, occupancy will increase through the better yield practice. The scientific measurement approach is the tool with which it can be precisely determined whether the occupancy increased because of the yield management practice or due to marketing programmes or improved economic conditions. It begins by identifying periods where the system does not restrict the hotel or resort in accepting bookings. This starts the process by which a look at what is occurring in the marketplace and in the local economy is gained. Scientific measurement isolates the impact of the marketing programmes and economic factors from the impact of the yield management solution. It shows what room revenue increases can be attributed to the yield management solution.

STRATEGIC LEVERS OF YIELD MANAGEMENT

Yield management, controlling customer demand through the use of variable pricing and capacity management to enhance profitability, has been examined extensively in the services literature. Most of this work has been tactical and mathematical rather than managerial. A broader view of yield management is valuable to both traditional and nontraditional users of the approach. Central to this broader view is the recognition of how different combinations of pricing and duration can be used as strategic levers to position service firms in their markets and the identification of tactics by which management can deploy these strategic levers. Further development of yield management requires that when the service is delivered be treated as a design variable that should be as carefully managed as the service process itself.

AN APPLICATION OF YIELD MANAGEMENT FOR INTERNET SERVICE PROVIDERS

This includes strategies for better utilizing the network capacity of Internet Service Providers (ISPs) when they are faced with stochastic and dynamic arrivals and departures of customers attempting to log-on or log-off, respectively. This proposes a method in which, depending on the number of modems available, and the arrival and departure rates of different classes of customers, a decision is made whether to accept or reject a logon request. The problem is formulated as a continuous time Markov Decision Process for which optimal policies can be readily derived using techniques such as value iteration. This decision maximizes the discounted value to ISPs while improving service levels for higher class customers. The methodology is similar to yield management techniques successfully used in airlines, hotels, etc. However, there are sufficient differences, such as no predefined time horizon or reservations, that make this model interesting to pursue and challenging.

FINITE HORIZON STOCHASTIC KNAPSACKS WITH APPLICATIONS TO YIELD MANAGEMENT

The finite horizon stochastic knapsack combines a secretary problem with an integer knapsack problem. It is useful for optimizing sales of perishable commodities with low marginal costs to impatient customers. Applications include yield management for airlines, hotels/motels, broadcasting advertisements, and car rentals. In these problems, K types of customers arrive stochastically. Customer type, k, has an integer weight w_k, a value b_k, and an arrival rate $y_k\,(t)$ (which depends on time). One considers arrivals over a continuous time horizon $[0; T]$ to a "knapsack" with capacity

W. For each arrival that fits in the remaining knapsack capacity, we may (1) accept it, receiving bk while giving up capacity wk; or (2) reject it, forgoing the value and not losing capacity. The choice must be immediate; a customer not accepted on arrival is lost. We model the problem using continuous time, discrete state, finite horizon, dynamic programming. We characterize the optimal return function and the optimal acceptance strategy for this problem, and we give solution methods. We generalize to multidimensional knapsack problems. We also consider the special case where $wk = 1$ for all k. This is the classic airline yield problem. Finally, we formulate and solve a new version of the secretary problem.

REVENUE AND YIELD MANAGEMENT IN HOTELS

Yield management is being practiced in airlines industry for the last 20 years and also in the hotels internationally for about 10 years. It basically applies to all retail sectors where capacity is fixed and enables the vendors like hotels to price the product differently for different market segments, purchase patterns and distribution channels. The basic objective is to increase the revenue and the contribution by charging a higher price from certain market segments, distribution channels, purchase patterns like length of advance booking etc. This is now being practiced very widely by all the hotel chains and progressive independent hotels for marketing of hotel room inventories. The strategy is designed to dramatically increase revenues, maximise profits, greatly improve the effectiveness of market segmentation, open new market segments and strengthen product portfolio strategies. The strategy and the implementation is dependent on having a good data about past purchases of different segments, occupancy levels in different parts of the year/parts of the week, occupancy achieved through different segments etc. There are sophisticated computer softwares and models available from the vendors, which are being used by all the practitioners. This course will give the general introduction, the concepts, implementation strategies and procedures. The concentration will be on implementation of these strategies for selling of hotel rooms, although some hotel chains and hotels are also implementing it for selling conference room spaces.

A course on "Revenue and Yield Management" should cover the concepts and strategies in the following areas:
- Introduction to Revenue Management: strategic policies.
- Yield Management: essentials of yield management, forecasting, demand based pricing, market segmentation, length of stay restrictions, choosing proper yield system for your organisation.

- Pricing: Methods of pricing like cost based pricing, perception pricing, demand based pricing and use of pricing as a strategic tool to increase profitability.
- Distribution: strategies to optimise exposure and manage multiple channels of distribution, impact of internet on distribution in hospitality industry and how to leverage it.
- Revenue Management Structure: implementation of revenue management structure, agenda and content, achieving change.

REVENUE MANAGEMENT AND YIELD MANAGEMENT IN HOTELS AND RESTAURANTS

Revenue management tends to be addressed from a marketing or operational perspective with few businesses considering the true effect on the "bottomline" of their yield management decisions. There have been attempts by writers to suggest a cost-oriented approach but this has been addressed from a technical, rather than a functional perspective. Most of the literature concentrates on operational decisions and does not address the supply of information to support these. This illustration seeks to identify some of the factors used in applying a cost-centred approach to revenue management and then to discuss the factors affecting this approach for managers from a financial management perspective. It is not the intention to look extensively at the marketing aspects which have been discussed exhaustively by previous authors, and so only a brief overview of the topic is given. Literature in the area of cost analysis and the provision of management information will be reviewed and consideration will also be given to the impact of technological change on the financial functions of the hotel business. The data presented will then be reviewed from a financial management perspective in order to discuss the implications for both operational and financial managers at the current time. Predictions for the impact of technological change on both revenue and financial management will also be presented to assist in identifying some of the challenges for the future in this area.

There have been many definitions of revenue management (RM). Many writers use the term interchangeably with yield management (YM) although some consider this relates to accommodation only whereas RM may encompass all areas of hotel revenue. Jauncey *et al.* (1995) define YM as being an "integrated, continuous and systematic approach to maximising rooms revenue." Early approaches to YM addressed only rooms revenue overall and it was only later that segmentation factors were included. This approach was informal and fairly unscientific but "almost always practiced by managers" (Bryant, 2000). The "father of Yield Management" (Bryant, 2000), Eric Orkin, first formally demonstrated in 1988 how calculations of the yield and a review of displacement could identify where gaps could be filled to increase occupancy. Me then developed his arguments to lead to staff "upselling" to maximise both average room rate and occupancy (Orkin, 1988). Two years later (Orkin, 1990) he also considered the profitability of different segments but only in the context of price-sensitivity. Revenue management is defined by-Cross (1997) as being "the application of disciplined tactics tha! predict consumer behaviour at the micro-market level" that will "maximise product availability and price" in order to maximise revenues. He looked at a range of industries, airlines being some of the major users of yield management techniques and having developed their systems in advance of other industries and hotels in particular. A number of studies have compared the operating performance of those adopting or not adopting yield management techniques (Jarvis et al., 1998). The multiplier effect was first discussed by Kimes (1989) who identified that just concentrating on rooms resulted in a hotel ignoring other revenue opportunities. She suggested that these should be incorporated into a full RM system hence not just maximising yield but revenues throughout Donaghy (1996) discusses the "improved financial performance' but refers only to revenue and Jones and Hamilton (1992) also do not consider the impact on other revenues or on profits. A review of the short break market (Edgar, 1997) identified that certain market segments offer much greater opportunities for maximising subsidiary revenues than others. This results in a RM approach (rather than yield) which attempts to identify which segments generate most revenues for the business as a whole, not just tor the rooms area. Cross (1997) uses simulation modelling to improve the "bottom line" but is actually discussing improving revenue rather than profits again the assumption that improved revenue automatically results in improved profits. However, his model could be adapted to include cost implications of the various products, or market segments. He does discuss "costing out the benefits" but implies these are just variable costs rather than all the cost of the particular transaction. He actively argues against taking a cost-oriented approach and focuses purely on revenue He suggests that tactics which result in sales increases or price "improvements" will have a greater impact on profits that those that focus on costs. He does not address the concept of both approaches being used together to ensure optimisation of profits.

The concept of the identification of costs, and hence maximisation of profit, has been discussed for some years. An approach towards considering rooms profitability was identified by Lockwood and Jones (1990) based on the "value-engineering' approach developed by Kasavana and Smith (1982). Lockwood and Jones identify two types of costs for a room servicing costs and raw materials. The first to consider a full market-segment approach were Dunn and Brooks (1990) who proposed a Market Segment Profitability Analysis approach (MSPA) which would drive staff to base their RM decisions on profitability rather than revenue maximisation. They recognised that certain departmental revenues are dependent on different (rooms) market segments and that the improvement of one may have a direct impact on the revenue, and eventually the profit, of another. Their major research suggested that what might appear to be a high-revenue segment might, when considering other revenue areas, be less productive of total profit than another with outwardly lower room prices. Costs need to be identified to support the YM decisions that are being made, not just for rooms (by segment) but for all ancillary revenue areas. These should include all support and fixed costs as well as the specific variable costs associated with delivering the product. This focuses on cost, as well as revenue management, would improve the contribution to hotel profits and increase the overall efficiency of the unit. Their approach was supported by Donaghy et al. (1995) who suggested a "yield focused approach" to the profitability of market segments which does identify all product costs which will then "add value" to the YM decision. A segmentation approach is essential, however, as different segments may incur different types of costs with marketing being quoted as an example. They do not, however, identify how these costs should be determined. Noone and Griffin (1997) consider that the information already provided by a YM system can form the basis for a Customer Profit Analysis (CPA) approach, with information being sourced from the property management system for each segment. This relates only to revenue, however, and so for cost information alternative approaches need to be considered. CPA is widely accepted but systems tend to analyse by product rather than customer, and this may not consider all relevant costs. They propose using Activity Based Costing (ABC) as a basis which identifies the type of task rather than the product ± for instance sales activities rather than sales salaries, telephone costs and so on. They suggest that overhead costs should be identified and then allocated to the respective market segment. They also suggest that certain types of customers consume far more costs than others, with the longer the stay, the lower the overhead costs per room night incurred (check in and out costs, for instance). There is a widescale-acceptance of the usefulness of ABC but a lack of usage in practice (Banerjee and Kane, 1996, in surveying managers from a variety of industries) and managers found it difficult to implement given the complexity of the data required for analysis. The key factor is technological systems which can analyse data and produce the required information in an understandable format and many more managers could use ABC if it were feasible. There is a clear identification of need here, but a lack of ability (and hence frustration) in terms of implementation. The use of ABC in the hotel industry has been minimal (Tai, 2000) with an informal survey by Graham (quoted in Tai, 2000) identifying no hotels in Europe that had adopted this approach. Tai interviewed a range of industry personnel in order to identify the reasons for this and found that, although there was considerable knowledge of the theory of ABC, there was a low understanding of how it might be used in a hotel context. Principal deterrents were seen as the complexity of the data required and the lack of systems to support accurate and timely analysis.

Further work by Gu and Canoon (1998) showed the application of modelling to produce estimations of contribution required from the various rooms rates. However they suggest that variable costs may be "easily based on cost standards for the room operation." This suggests that standard costing techniques are used and that strong controls are made on the variable costs of the various departments, whereas in reality these may be less controllable than anticipated. However, in practice, hotels are diverse in character with a wide variety of cost structures (Harris, 1999) and so use of industry-wide standards may not be feasible. However, usage of budgeted costs, planned for the specific individual unit, may well be appropriate if the information can be accurately determined in the required format.

One of the key issues when addressing the use of costs in RM decisions is the need for suitable information and its availability from modern computer systems. The need for accounting information for marketing decisions has been researched by Downie (1996) who has demonstrated that managers first need to identify what type of decisions are made and the specific type of information. The inference is drawn that, if the emphasis is placed on the profitability of their decisions in other words, they take a financially-oriented approach then they will contribute to the profitability of the establishment and not just the revenue (or the costs). She also concludes that information should be geared to the future rather than the past, so that the manager considers impending decisions rather than just reflecting on past performance. This approach, whilst initially focusing on the general marketing function, is obviously appropriate for those involved in RM. The critical success factors (CSFs) in hospitality were identified by Jones (1991) who found that the two key areas were a good computer system and internal control procedures. Up-to-date information was the third most important feature and the measures most used by managers to assess CSFs were the analysis of financial data and weekly forecasts. Goussak (1995) suggests that systems have developed somewhat haphazardly and that there has been a lack of strategic planning in systems sections have been "added-on" piecemeal. A comprehensive review needed to take place to ensure future reliability and the identification of risk. These findings were supported by Teare and Bowen (1997) who also found a lack of strategic focus in planning hotel-wide systems. Other writers (Cross, 1997; Jarvis *et al.*, 1998; Hanson and Eringa, 1998; Puchik, 2000) highlight the need for both qualitative and quantitative data and confirm that this is only practical with sophisticated systems. The model developed by Gu and Canoon (1998) factors in such items as seasonaliry, disposable income, service quality and competition, just to enhance room rates. They suggest that, once cost data has been included, the requirements of an information system become almost impossibly complex and multidimensional. This approach has also been considered by McEvoy (1997). Recently Wang (2000) has tentatively proposed a theoretical model which will utilise both market segmentation and ABC / MSPA to categorise those segments that result in higher profits and hence need increased information and management, although this has not yet been tested in practice. It is clear that, without sophisticated technological systems, it is not possible to accurately identify the costs relevant to each market segment. The information required is complex and requires a full analysis of actual expenditure, by segment, over a period of time. Utilisation of the Uniform System of Accounts for Lodging (International Association of Hospitality Accountants, 1996) gives a standard approach to presenting data but this is designed only for the overall rooms area and not for individual segments (apart from revenues, which may be shown separately). Development of the USAL to provide full financial statements by market segment would facilitate a profit-based RM approach.

There appears to be widespread awareness of the principle of CPA in hospitality and acceptance of the need to adopt a cost-centred approach, but minimal usage in practice. Given that one of the prime deterrents appears to be the lack of systems to cope with the detailed analysis of data, discussion of some of the future technological trends in the area may give some insight into future strategy. The major influence on the provision of information is now seen as the worldwide web (Jeong and Lambert, 1999). In the past this has been used for marketing and communications functions but is now expanding for a wide variety of business uses. The type of reservations facilities now available via the Web have four main features checking availability, making reservations, securing reservations and receiving confirmation (Book-hotel, 2000) all very much focused on the booking process rather than providing a detailed service for customers. These need to be clearly linked into Global Distribution Systems (GDSs),

(Hot-key 2000) to ensure that the hotel can optimise the use of the Web, as well as the customer. Integration of systems has been slow and expensive and many companies still do not appear to have a clear strategic direction about the role of technology in their future success (Cline, 1999). In 1999, 3.1 per cent of revenues were estimated to be spent on average on technology, and this was predicted to rise to 4 per cent in 2000. This expenditure is primarily on PMS (property management systems) with YM being seen as secondary rather than a holistic view of full integration being considered. The integration of PMS and CRS has been very slow indeed although by the end of 2000 the vast majority of companies should have achieved this. However, YM systems are not always integrated to property management or central reservation systems which appears to complicate the processes and hence increase the potential for both for error and costs. For the future, the business-to-customer (B2C) approach will prevail (Richards, 2000) which will provide not just a booking service but an entire customer-focused service approach. For the hotel, this will include GDS management but also provide products and services applied to customers as individuals, not just as a homogeneous group, which should build loyalty as well as revenues. The development of Web technology as a resource for all managers and in particular for a full e-commerce service was still some way ahead, with a lack of understanding by senior managers as to the scope of systems to enhance the skills and information of all managers (O'Connor and Horan, 1999). Additionally, future changes in Web technology will improve the transfer of data between computers (Classe, 2000) by eliminating the need for expensive interfaces or re-analysis of data. The information gained from guests can be "mined" (Berkus, 2000; Troutman, 1999) to give detailed information on all aspects of guest lifestyle and expenditure within the property. It seems feasible, therefore, that these systems could be extended to include a detailed analysis of guest expenditure by market segment, so satisfying some of the needs of a MSPA approach. If these individual guest spends could then be costed then a full profit-per-segment could emerge. Instant distribution of information will allow instant usage by relevant managers, providing it is presented in a format which they can use and understand.

The Role of Finance

Much of the YM/RM literature has concentrated on the Front Office areas with little consideration of the contribution of other managers, particularly the finance function. Hanson and Eringa (1998) have suggested that the conventional approach to YM is that it concerns the front office area only. They discuss the need for YM to be considered a "hotel-wide effort" and that the Yield Manager should be a co-ordinator of all those functions which impact on the objectives of the YM programme. They tend to ignore the finance function although there are implicit suggestions of the contribution that can be made. The human element in effective YM is "crucial." The need for a team approach to YM is also considered by Donaghy *et al.* (1995) who also identify the need for a team approach which utilises the cost and revenue awareness of all in order to improve decision making, and hence profits. Joint consultation is essential between accounts staff and managers (Tjosvold and Poon, 1998) if informed and productive decision making is to occur, with a consequent improvement in efficiency and hence profits. Although managers may hold opposing views the identification and exploration of these may be productive and assist in solving problems to the benefit of all departments. This may be interpreted on behalf of the YM area where the involvement of the finance function in YM discussions enhances the information product and hence the decisions agreed with consequent benefit for all parties. Discussions held among financial personnel (Burgess, 2000a) have shown that, in their opinion, technology will continue to change the operation of the hotel with resulting changes in both costs and management required. Financial managers will need to provide a high level of information to operational areas and, with increasing responsibility for systems management within their hotel, this will include developing and implementing new processes to ensure that only information that is necessary to, and usable by, managers, is issued. Further focus group discussions (Burgess, 2000b) also identified a level of concern about the involvement of the finance function in operational decisions. Although financial managers were conscious of the need to become more knowledgeable about operational areas, and technology-driven topics in particular, there was still some resistance from operational managers as to a perceived "interference." However, the supply of information was crucial to all managers in better performance of their jobs, and the finance function is seen as paramount in this provision. Other research (Burgess, 1999) also showed that the financial manager was crucial to the effective operation of the business, and that managers wished to become much more involved, and knowledgeable, about the operational and technological functions so as to be aware of the potential problems and facilitate solutions. There is a desire by financial managers to contribute to decision making by providing the necessary information and support to the operational areas. "Knowledge management" (Graham, 1999) will become increasingly important and this is likely to be managed by the finance area, all of which suggest that the role of the financial manager in revenue management decisions is crucial.

The Contribution of the Financial Manager to Revenue Management and Profitability

RM has developed from early YM techniques to considering a full MSPA approach. However, developments in this area have been largely theoretical and little practical progress has been achieved. The main reason for this has been the complexity of the information required if accurate decisions are to be made. The need for information is apparent, it is the supply that is problematic. Analysis of costs has in the past been largely based on departmental statements with little attempt to allocate these to different types of customer, or market segments. ABC is one technique that has been considered extensively in theory but has proved impossible to implement in practice. The opportunity is now emerging to utilise modem technology to identify the relevant costs, by customer, and then to produce market-segment based information in order to achieve a full Customer Profit Analysis. The impending improvements in the transfer of data should make this process easier and cost-effective. However, these are technical approaches and consideration should also be made of the human implications of improving financial information. The finance area has developed a key role in providing information for managers and this becomes more critical as the need increases. The financial manager is also frequently responsible for systems management within the hotel and projected improvements in technology will impact directly on their responsibilities the B2C approach. It is no longer possible to consider RM as a function solely of the front office area it now involves many other areas of management, and finance in particular. If the optimum profitability from customers is to be achieved then careful planning, including the design of systems, needs to be made by all involved personnel. A team approach to RM is essential. In conclusion, the finance area has had little involvement in RM decisions in the past, due to the emphasis being placed on revenues rather than profits. Improved technology will result in improved financial information which will in turn facilitate RM decisions to optimise profits from all customers. The finance area has a key role to play in designing and implementing cost management systems approaches to enable this to take place.

REVENUE MANAGEMENT

In the last few decades, passenger reservations systems have evolved from low level inventory control processes to major strategic information systems. Today, airlines and other transportation companies view revenue management systems and related information technologies as critical determinants of future success. Indeed, expectations of revenue gains that are possible with expanded revenue management capabilities are now driving the acquisition of new information technology. Each advance in information technology creates an opportunity for more comprehensive reservations control and greater integration with other important transportation planning functions,

Background

Before 1972, almost all quantitative research in reservations control focused on controlled overbooking. The overbooking calculations depended on predictions of the probability distributions of the number of passengers who appeared for boarding at flight time, so overbooking research also stimulated useful research on disaggregate forecasting of passenger cancellations, no-shows, and go-shows. Both forecasting and controlled overbooking achieved a moderate degree of success and established a degree of credibility for scientific approaches to reservations control. In the early 1970s, some airlines began offering restricted discount fare products that mixed discount and higher fare passengers in the same aircraft compartments. For example, BOAC (now British Airways) offered earlybird bookings that charged lower fares to passengers who booked at least twenty-one clays in advance of flight departure. This innovation offered the airline the potential of gaining revenue from seats that would otherwise fly empty; however, it presented them with the problem of determining the number of seats thai should be protected for late booking, full fare passengers. If too few seats were protected, the airline would spill full fare passengers; if too many were protected, flights would depart with empty seats. No simple rule, like protecting a fixed percentage of capacity, could be applied across all flights because passenger booking behaviour varied widely with relative fares, itineraries, season, day of week, time of day, and other factors. It was evident that effective control of discount seats would require detailed tracking of booking histories, expansion of information system capabilities, and careful research and development of seat inventory control rules. Littlewood (1972) of BOAC proposed that discount fare bookings should be accepted as long as their revenue value exceeded the expected revenue of future full fare bookings. This simple, two fare, seat inventory control rule (henceforth, Littlewood's rule) marked the beginning of what came to be called yield management and, later, revenue management. In North America, the beginning of intensive development of revenue management techniques dates from the launch of American Airlines' Super Saver fares in April of 1977, shortly before the deregulation of US domestic and international airlines. Over the last twenty years, development of revenue management systems has progressed from simple single leg control, through segment control, and finally to origin-destination control. Each of these advances has required investment in more sophisticated information systems, but the return on these investments has been excellent [see, for example, Smith, Leimkuhler, and Darrow (1992), Cross (1995)]. In 1999, most of the world's major air carriers and many smaller airlines have some level of revenue management capability. Other small airlines and international airlines in newly deregulated markets are beginning the development process. The success of airline revenue management was widely reported, and this stimulated development of revenue management systems for other transportation sectors and in other areas of the service sector.

Airline Revenue Management Problem

The objective in revenue management is to maximize profits, however, airline short-term costs are largely fixed, and variable costs per passenger are small; thus, in most situations, it is sufficient to seek booking policies that maximize revenues. Also, although there is lower risk in accepting a current booking request than in waiting for later possible bookings, booking decisions are repeated millions of times per year; therefore, a risk-neutral approach is justified. All of our discussion in this section will assume risk neutral maximization of expected revenues as the objective. Consider the arrival of a booking request that requires seats in an itinerary—one or more flights departing and arriving at specified times, within a specific booking class, at a given fare. The fundamental revenue management decision is whether or not to accept or reject this booking. Durham (1995) reports that a large computer reservations systems must handle five thousand such transactions per second at peak times, thus the decision must be reached within milliseconds of the request's arrival. Not surprisingly, no current revenue management system attempts full assessment of each booking request in real time. Instead, precomputed aggregate control limits are set that will close the system for further bookings of specific types while leaving it open for others. The reservations system can quickly determine the open or closed status of a booking category and report back to an agent or customer without actually evaluating the request. The accept-reject decision can be restated as a question of valuation: What is the expected displacement cost of closing the incremental seats in the requested itinerary? To maximize expected revenues, the request should be satisfied only if the fare value of the requested itinerary equals or exceeds the expected displacement cost. The apparent simplicity of this valuation problem is deceptive—a complete assessment must allow for all possible future realizations of the reservations process that could be influenced by the availability of any of the seats on any of the legs in the booking. Fully traced, this influence propagates across the entire airline network because a booking can displace potential bookings that will have subsequent impacts of their own. This influence also propagates forward in time because many affected itineraries will terminate later than the booking being considered. Also, a booking will normally have a return component at a later date with its own set of concurrent and downstream effects. Many other factors increase the complexity of the evaluation process. The practical complexities of revenue management are daunting—we do not have space here to discuss all of them. As is always true, modelling, theoretical analyses, and implementation rely on assuming away many of these complicating factors and approximating others. It is important to remember that such approximations have yielded enormous revenue benefits for airlines and other enterprises. The performance of a given revenue management system depends, in large part, on the frequency and accuracy of updates to control limits and the number of distinct booking classes that can be controlled. The determination of suitable control limits and characterization of their structural properties over time has been the principal focus of academic research, whereas the need for practical and implementable approximations to optimal limits has driven much of the practitioner research.

Table 1: Elements of Airline Revenue Management

Customer Behaviour and Demand Forecasting	Revenue Factors
Demand volatility	Fare values
Seasonally, day-of-week variation	Uncertainty of fare value
Special events	Frequent flyer redemptions
Sensitivity to pricing actions	Company or travel agent special vouchers
Demand dependencies between booking classes	Cancellation penalties or restrictions
Return itineraries	Variable Cost Factors
Batch bookings	Marginal costs per passenger
Cancellations	Denied boarding penalties
Censorship of historical demand data	Goodwill costs
Defections from delayed flights	Fare Products
Diversions	Number of products
Go-Shows	Fences (restrictions)

Group bookings	Problem Scale
Interspersed arrivals e.g., United/Lufthansa/SAS ORION System:	Large airline or airline alliance;
No-shows itineraries/day [see GARVEY (1997),	4,000 flights and 350,000 passenger
Recapture	BOYD (1998)]
Upgrades	Problem Interfaces
Control System	Market strategy
Booking lead time (often 300 days or more)	Code-sharing alliances
Number of controllable booking classes	Routing

CRM—Return on Investment (ROI)

Quantifying how much revenue is generated or costs saved as a result of employing CRM is difficult, A firm's operational systems are more straightforward and deliver, for the most part, defined outcomes and measurable improvements. On the other hand, CRM initiatives often foster the formation and development of unprecedented business practices that are by their nature difficult to quantify. Exacerbating the problem is that many CRM svstems were planned and executed during the late 1990's—IT's heyday for rampant spending on technology without much cost justification. During these tougher economic times, however, most executives are requiring careful cost-benefit analysis up front before making the decision to deploy CRM in their company. The best approach to defining the correct mix of ROl metrics is to identify the benefits sought from CRM before is inception and out of that—proclamation of the stated benefits will naturally flow the right strategic and tactical measures to keep the CRM initiative on track.

The basic method for defining CRM ROI is from cost savings and revenue generation. For example, CRM can result in revenue or cost savings represented in a broad range of metrics such as campaign-expense reduction: when prospective targets are selected more effectively, campaign volumes decline and expense-to-revenue ratios fall: internal process improvements: the percentage of customer orders that can be handled automatically, shorter sales-cycle time and less rework, and service centre efficiency: when the duration of a transaction or a problem resolution call is shorten, that translates directly into lower head-count requirements. SBC Communications is a good example of CRM ROI. SBC's Easy Access Sales Environment, an on-line tool to help customer support representatives, costs $34.2 million. The tool helped sales representatives access product information faster and pull in more comprehensive customer data, allowing an increase in call volume, a simultaneous decrease in call duration, and improved order accuracy. All told, the estimated ROI for the Easy Access Sales Environment was revealed to be 4483.6 million.

Often times briefing C-level managers on cost savings is easier than reporting on the benefits associated with increased revenues. Metropolitan Life's Alien Harris, VP of Technical Services, claims that many CEO's are a little suspicious of assigning any causality to revenue increase and that revenue itself is too vague to justify investments. Met Life, subsequently, focuses on operational efficiencies garnered through CRM like consolidating service centres and eliminating redundancy. Harris' team identified very specific areas when costs would disappear. They kept track of how problems were resolved in their call centres, how much time resolution took, and how many people were involved. If they saw an increase in the number of problems resolved at a single point of customer contact, then they knew they were going in the right direction.

Even though they sell their CRM projects based on cost reduction, most markets anticipate that revenue increase will follow their efforts. Automating marketing processes is usually about efficiency, meaning cost saving and is more palatable for managers in finance. However, outcomes based on CRM should be economic, not operational, and ultimately, profit is the number one metric. Revenue increases from CRM can flow from a number of sources:

- Campaign-response improvements which yields more orders and more new customers
- Increased average order size or the number of products purchased in an order
- Competitive wins, like an increase in the share of the customer's wallet
- Customer profitability—migrating customer groups from lower to higher value levels

However, revenue enhancements that measure CRM ROI may be problematic in that they can take a long time to materialize because revenue is dependent on sales cycles, the size of the organization, and the amount of behavioural change needed in the company. Dallas-based Credit Union of Texas ($1 Billion in assets) uses a revenue-based CRM ROI. The Credit Union looks at internal operational enhancements, but most of their focus is external based on acquiring new members, increased sales, and improved marketing utilizing BI and trend analysis. The Credit Union's first campaign objective was to raise the profitability of the 44,000 low value members the bank was serving. These accounts carried low balances and subscribed to only one-bank service. With CRM analysis, the Credit Union identified which of the institutions services were most likely to interest each low-value customer. Subsequently, a personalized direct-mail campaign with three different offerings to each customer garnered a substantial 10.4 response rate in just four months. 2,272 customers signed up for additional services, resulting in $150,000 additional net profit. Another 3,600 decided to close their accounts, which saved the bank $73,000 in service costs. The campaign itself cost only $45,000, and the Credit Union plans follow-up mailings to offer a different set of service options to non-responders or the chance to close their accounts altogether. The campaign's net present value was over $335,000.

Companies adopting CRM because of the cost savings it promises may have problems justifying their case. With the escalating complexity and pricing of many CRM products, seeing a return of investment might take a few years. The real justification for CRM goes back to improving the customer's experience with the corporation, humanizing this experience, and making it easier to do business. CRM is about managing and monitoring customer relationships and increasing their value. It is about motivating customers to tell their friends and relatives to buy a particular firm's products.

Therefore, the best metrics for measuring CRM ROI revolve around the customer themselves. Three important measures track:

- Customer satisfaction
- Customer attrition
- Customer life-time value (CLV)

Customer satisfaction can be measured by observing behaviour, but it is more likely to be captured by utilizing surveys. Satisfaction should be evaluated around the customer's relationship with an entire product brand, versus a single production or function.

Customer attrition—means measuring churn rates compared to industry bench-marks. Attrition is best analyzed by segment, since customer value can vary widely. Simply put, CLV is calculated as the revenues the customer will generate over the life of their relationship with a company, net of the variable cost of achieving these sales (the cost of goods sold) and the cost to serve. Historically, CRM efforts are targeted at attracting new customers and retaining, up selling, or cross selling to existing customers. Revenue is the most frequently used metric in measuring the success of these efforts. Yet, companies are increasingly asking questions such as: Are these our most profitable customers? Are these the customers to whom ! should devote my scarce and costly sales and service resources? Is revenue alone an adequate measure of customer value? CLV can help answer these questions. It is a performance measure of long-term customer worth. David Coppock (2002), author on several applications of CLV, explains that CLV is the expected value of profit to a business derived from customer relationships from the present to some future point in time (usually three years out). Mr. Coppock contends that CLV does not include past contributions to profit, but it is probabilistic in that CLV may be used to increase future profitability.

Coppock (2002) reveals a cable company's model for increasing CLV. Present value over 24 months of [{(direct profit per month of basic service)* (profitability that the household is still a customer) + (profit from premium service)* (probability that the household upgrades service) + profit of pay-per-view purchases)* (expected number of pay-per-view purchases)} * (probability that households do not default on bill)-(cost of service calls)* (probability that a household will require a service call)].

The paramount issue is that CLV analysis rolls up the elements of revenue, expense, and customer behaviour that drive profitability into one quantifiable metric. In addition, the CLV metric involves the essential marketing aspects of retention, cross-selling credit risk, pricing, and expense evaluation. As an example oi CLV, suppose a company spends $1 million on an e-mail campaign and sent to 100,000 qualified e-mail addresses. The cost of the e-mail list is $1,000 per thousand addresses. In doing some research, the company determines that the click through rate of 5½ per cent on e-mailing. This situation generates 5,500 sales at $69.95 for a particular product. Historically, the CLV of customers acquired through e-mail is a total expenditure of $400 and a profit of $80 per customer. By dividing the $1 million dollars by 5,500, the acquisition cost of each customer is $181.81. The revenue generated from the sale of 5,500 product X at $69.95 each is $384,725. At face value there appears to be a $615,275 loss—cost of the campaign minus the revenue generated. However, each of these customers, due to anticipated CLV, will generate $440,000 in profit with gross revenue of $2.2 million. The idea is that customers are tracked through their life term with the company—the number of years determined by marketers.

Mei Lin Fung (2001), Managing Director at Wainscott Venture Partners, uses CLV methodologies extensively in funding venture capital for high-tech start-ups. Ms. Fung's approach is to measure the cost of acquisition, selling costs, customer care cost, and revenue. The net profit is then calculated for the most profitable customers. The top tier of profitable customers is closely examined, with special attention being paid to how they were acquired. Most companies would be surprised with the result. Ms. Fung claims that the most valuable lend generating activities occur by chance and not by design. Some are replicable, some are not. Ms. Fung suggests that managers observe the lead generators that use replicable and design programmes to report the process. In addition, it is important for managers to describe the most profitable customers that the corporation would like to have, and determine what it will take to get them. Lastly, Ms. Fung recommends that managers define the acquisition, selling and customer care process, and calculate the ROI on the ideal customers that are worth acquiring. After checking that these customers have the potential to be profitable, managers can then identify the most profitable leads. Lead generation is predicated on a sales pipeline plus an awareness factor that anticipates the level of sales needed to obtain a goal. Consequently, historical data identifies the number of leads or opportunities needed to achieve objectives. Therefore, customer relationships become quantified rather than amorphous and objectives clear rather than vague. Once CLV is established, it may be easier to design programmes that can escalate the customer type's CLV that can take the form of increased revenue from the customer through up selling and cross selling.

In conclusion, it appears that as companies struggle with short-term efficiency measures and long-term revenue and customer measures, one aspect is clear: the average CRM project is difficult to justify based on a classical analysis. According to a Hewson Consulting Group (2001) study, most investments in CRM have been a matter of faith—a large percentage had no formal cost-benefit justification. However, due to CRM analysis, marketers are able to track the success rate of a particular campaign with multiple opportunities to drill down through data to see who, what, when, where, and how a campaign is successful. The metrics for success in marketing RO1 identify the more profitable customers through the use of CLV, more revenue derived from more highly focused types or campaigns, improved cost savings, and improved product and service profitability.

The Future of CRM

With the increased penetration of CRM philosophies in organizations and concomitant rise in spending on people and products to implement them, it appears that there will be improvements in how companies work to establish long-term relationships with their customers. More companies are recognizing the importance of creating CRM databases and are getting creative at capturing customer information. Real-time analyses of customer behaviour on the web for better customer selection and targeting is currently possible. This real-time access permits companies to anticipate what customers are likely to buy. Real-time information is made possible through the use of real-time data warehousing and associated analytics.

Another development in the realm of CRM is the establishment of a C-level officer, Chief Customer Officer (CCO), who is relegated to developing an improved focus on CRM and how CRM is used to take care of customers. The CCO's job is to provide intelligence to higher-level executives from marketing research and the customer database for use by product managers in formulating marketing plans and making decisions. In addition, the CCO's manages the customer service operation. The CCO also interacts with other company managers whose operations may have a direct impact on customer satisfaction. The CCO at Equalfooting.com, a company offering streamlined purchasing, financing, and shipping services for small manufacturing and construction businesses, has the job of integrating marketing and operations to make sure that customers are satisfied.

Another development involving CRM is the notion of customer satisfaction being expanded to change CRM to CEM, Customer Experience Management. The idea behind this is that with the number of customer contact points increasing all the time, it is more critical than ever to measure the customer's reactions to these contacts and to develop immediate responses to negative experiences. These responses could include timely apologies and special offers to compensate for unsatisfactory service. The objective is to expand the notion of a relationship from one that is transaction-based to one that is experimental and continuous. Info World editor, Paul Krill (2002), reports that some companies are outsourcing their CRM projects. Mr. Krill reveals that outsourcing usually increases during troubled economic times as companies try to control costs. In addition, companies considering CRM applications also realize that deploying a CRM system is resource intensive and has a high-failure rate attached to its implementation. Subsequently, firms are willing to outsource CRM to the experts. For example, Nextel expects to save $1 billion during the next eight years by hiring IBM to handle its CRM applications so that Nextel can concentrate on its core competency of managing networks while leaving customer relationship to the outsourcer. It appears that outsourcing CRM will continue to grow as companies realize cost savings on infrastructure, software, and staff, as well as providing a venue for faster development. The future of CRM will also invite personalized access for customers via a web-based portal. Portals provide integration of several customer facing systems, and it gives users the ability to personalize the flow of data and analytics to any role inside or outside the company. mCRM or Mobile CRM is another promising CRM development. mCRM is a wireless/mobile CRM that allows two-way interactivity between the customer and the vendor continuously—anywhere and anytime. CRM aspects such as customer service, customer acquisition, customer retention, and market analysis will be processed through hand-held or similar wireless devices. KnowEx is a wireless pioneer that has developed a mobile system—KnowEx Wireless 2.5 eCRM solution that provides a secure chat, data based integration, streaming media so that users can easily access customer service histories. Soon, sales people will be able to close a deal on site, give specific guidance as to availability, place an order on their Palm Pilot, and have it not only registered in the CRM system back at the home office, but also to trigger manufacturing and billing and having the product shipped in an instant—at the speed of the Internet. Natural language speech recognition, and interactive voice response (IVR) are also important to the future of CRM. The transformation of call centres with some IVR to full-service, multimedia-based customer interaction centres is on the horizon. More sophisticated IVR systems that ask for identification that is transmitted verbally read back by voice and then queried against a table that identities the number as belonging to the customer and responds appropriately will be available soon. In addition, IVR CRM systems of the future will provide complete integration of voice data, using multimedia across multiple channels to route a call or inquiry to the appropriate call centre within the company. IVR systems, while not substitutes for live customer care representatives, could be used to satisfy the needs of less profitable or lower maintenance customers. Related to IVR is the idea of customer self-help CRM systems. Web-based systems allow customers to browse the company's knowledge centre to help solve problems that they may have. Customers can also check on the status of previous inquiries and submit new ones. In addition, self-help CRM systems save companies money by solving routine problems through the use of e-mail, interactive chat, web portals, and on-line knowledge databases instead of using more expensive, live customer care agents.

Privacy Issues Regarding CRM

Privacy issues involving customer information have come into light recently with the repercussions surrounding the Toysmart and Double Click debacle. Issues surrounding selling customer data to other companies or merging customer information and anonymous user activity have e-businesses coping with the probability of increased government intervention as to the privacy implications surrounding the handling of customer data. Of pure consequence for companies that have CRM is the delicate balancing act between personalization and privacy. Copious amounts of customer data are collected, analyzed, and shared to provide customization and a favourable experience. However, the customer must know how the data is being used and how to evoke their rights when its use is not fully disclosed. Many companies are providing the customer with a choice as to how their personal data is used by initiating "opt-in" or permission-based marketing. A favoured approach to customer data and privacy is to begin dialogue with their customers to make them aware of their own privacy rights and how to exercise them. Many customers do not know the difference between identity theft and privacy violations. Identity theft is stealing personal data to commit a crime. The greatest risks to a customer are privacy violations (like selling personal data) and, therefore, consumers are more likely to take out of context the limited information they do have, especially from bad press. To avoid problems regarding privacy issues while trying to deploy CRM, managers need to:

- Motivate customers to share information by providing something in return, such as providing e-mailed discount coupons for future purchases for registering at the company's site.
- Ensure privacy policy is conspicuously posted on web sites, e-mails, call centres, and every touch point where customer data is collected.
- Consider giving customers full access to information that is already collected on them, thus allowing the customer to manage this information.
- Regard every customer's privacy preference and ensure that the preference becomes integrated into all aspects, databases, and processes throughout the company's CRM system.
- Make marketers responsible for enforcing customer privacy policies, standards, and rules and have them communicate the policies, both internally and externally.
- Follow the guidelines revealed by the FTC regarding privacy issues and information practices of notice, choice, access, and control.

The bottom line regarding privacy issues and CRM is that companies might lose business if customers do not trust that personal information will be carefully guarded. Many consumers abandon their "shopping cart" because on-line companies are not clear about their privacy policies. In addition, many CRM systems may be affected by the enforcement of recent laws, most notably, the Gramm-Leach-Bliley Services Modernization Act and the Health Insurance Portability and Accountability Act (H1PAA). The Gramm-Leach-Bliley is forcing companies to "clean" their customer data so that the data matches across all business functions and processed. This situation allows privacy preferences (such as "opt-in") to be consistently applied throughout the organization. HIPAA restricts access to customer data on a need-to-know basis, thus databases must be restructured throughout the firm to allow this granularity of access. When customers know how their data is being controlled and managed, it gives them a feeling of security and trust—the basis for good customer relations and effective management of CRM.

Conclusion

In general CRM solutions attempt to establish relationships with customers on an individual basis and then use the information gathered from this relationship to treat different customers differently. The mutual exchange between a customer and company becomes mutually beneficial. Customers receive the shopping and service experience that they deserve; the provider receives ongoing loyalty resulting in increased business. The key here is customer loyalty and more specifically, customer lifetime value. BI analytics allows companies to evaluate the profitability of each customer transaction and compare it against their expected lifetime value. The age-old (almost cliche) 80/20 rule where 80 per cent of customer service and other associated costs are created by 20 per cent of a firm's customers is still viable. Subsequently, companies will react accordingly by directing all but the most valuable customers to an automated e-mail and voice-response system. Furthermore, even as companies weigh customers through the lens of profitability, customers will likewise evaluate companies on their service levels. Companies that can provide good service cheaply and efficiently will probably win customer loyalty. Price will be a motivator; however, the Internet has made pricing almost transparent, making significant differentiation more difficult. Consequently, excellent service and delivery will become the hallmark of successful e-Businesses, especially those who have interactive web sites. As in the real world, convenience is an increasing factor in where an on-line customer elects to shop for all but the most specialized of goods. However, with the aspect of customer loyalty and customer lifetime value being a paramount factor for many e-Business CRM projects, there appears to be a contradiction in the importance of loyal customers when compared to acquiring new ones. Recent studies have down that customer acquisition costs have dropped by nearly 50 per cent in the last year. In addition, both e-mail and permission marketing spending will increase two-fold from

2001-2002. And, the customer acquisition to retention dollars spent has risen nearly four times in the past year. This situation is contradictory to what most research has shown— repeat customers spend significantly more per purchase than new customers. Even more perplexing is trying to determine if CRM does in fact increase the bottom line of e-Businesses. Research has shown that between 50 to 70 per cent of CRM initiatives do not produce many measurable business benefits or fail completely (www.cio.com, 2002). Yet spending on CRM systems will increase from $20.4 billion in 2001 to $46 billion in 2003 (www.crmguru.com, 2002)! In addition, according to a recent Information Week Study, 24 per cent of companies with CRM implementations underway or planned say they will spend between $1-$5 million in the next 12 months on those projects, and 13 per cent will spend more than $5 million. Of course, spending depends on a company's size: a majority of small companies will spend less than $100,000 in the next year, while 57 per cent mid-size companies will spend between $100,000 and $1 million, and 72 per cent of large companies will spend more than $1 million. One problem with measuring the success of CRM systems is that traditional ROI metrics just do not work for CRM. Traditional accounting measures do not easily lend themselves to comparing things that involve "time series" data. However, CLV ROI measures allow companies to measure beyond a one-time period and one customer. CLV analysis combines accounting principles of discounted cash flow and activity based costing, along with actuarial probabilities for customer retention and other forecasting approaches to help a company understand the financial impact of different CRM scenarios. However, CLV for CRM applications is a relatively new concept, and it is not widely accepted as a ROI metric yet. According to the research, the companies who have failed (e.g. stopped the project) CRM deployments usually have "failure factors" in common:

- Not accurately estimating costs, especially the costs associated with the consultants necessary to deploy these systems. A majority of the cost of implementing a CRM system is attributed to training, installation, integration, and customization—all of which is related to consultants

- The majority of the end- users of the CRM system rejected it— especially Sales Force Automation implementations It appears most sales people relied on the old way of doing business and were too strung out to learn a new system In addition, if employees feel CRM will threaten their jobs (i.e., automated call centre resolution system) they might be inclined to tell customers to not use it.

- Internal resistance to sharing customer information from business function to business function. Departments within corporations traditionally have become silos of information. Without key management intervention and diplomacy, information will stay departmentalized.

The companies who have successfully met their CRM objectives usually have these "success factors" in common

- Companies had a clear vision as to why there were employing a CRM system, whether it was employed to let the customers' needs drive the system, or if it was employed to increase customer loyalty. A clear vision to its implementation was stated and disseminated throughout the company.
- There was a champion—whether CEO, CCO, or CIO who was determined to see the successful implementation of the CRM system.
- There was evidence of a business process re-engineering taking place that resulted in the way the business viewed its customers. In other words, create one system and one view to track all customers at all touch points.
- The best of breed application suite approach versus the all-encompassing ERP-like systems appeared to be more successful, especially when pilot programmes were run in phases. Enterprise integration is an essential element to CRM; however, its application is difficult and expensive to undertake. In addition, no one retailer of CRM systems has developed an application that covers all aspects of CRM.
- The management of change seems to help the implementation of CRM. Flattening out the organizational structure, rewriting job descriptions, developing new business processes, eliminating redundancy, and rethinking system requirements appear to be key to CRM success.
- Sometimes a second or third CRM implementation attempt works. Companies with deep pockets learned lessons from previous failed attempts at CRM deployment.

The bottom line is whether or not CRM has favourably impacted e-Business. The short answer is yes, it has. However, as previously stated, it is difficult to measure the- success of a CRM deployment. The list of the best suppliers of (RM systems include:

- People Soft (www.pcopiesoft.com)
- Onyx (www.onyx.com)
- Siebel (www.siebel.com)
- Nortel (wwvv.nortel.com)
- Micro Strategy (www.microstrategy.com)
- Oracle (www.oracle.com)
- E-piphany (www.epiphany.com)
- Pivotal (www. pivotal.com)
- Broad vision (www.broadvision.com)

These suppliers have helped the likes of Ford, Tavlor Made, Boise Cascade, Vanguard, American Express, L.L. Bean, Charles Schwab, AT&T, AOL, Ayaia, BMW, Dell, SBC, Sears, Eddie Bauer, Member Works, Office Furniture.com, and many others who make their e-Business endeavours more successful through the use of an effective CRM initiative. What it really boils down to is that these companies are willing to take care of loyal customers and to become more customer centric. Subsequently, they are able to enjoy the rewards of their vision and efforts.

Relationship Management

The original focus of CRM was to forge closer and. deeper relationships with customers, being willing and able to change your behaviour toward an individual customer based on what the customer tells you and what else you know about the customer. The premise being that existing customers are more profitable than new customers; that it is less expensive to sell an incremental product to an existing customers; customer retention would be maximised by matching products and levels of service more closely to customer expectations; and attracting new customers is expensive. The central objective of CRM is thus to maximise the lifetime value of a customer to the organisation.

The evidence of having superior customer relationships is overwhelming.

- Relationship marketing increases retention. Research highlights that high levels of customer satisfaction are associated with increased retention of customers.
- Relationship builds more easily when there is two-way communication—and where organisations set up feed back loops, there is their potential to learn from customers.

- Relationship behaviour anticipates customer demands. By engaging in an interactive dialogue customer preferences can be determined.
- Retained customers are inevitably more profitable. The research is clear that it costs much more to attract a new customer as it does to retain an existing customer; and that existing customers are more profitable. A knock-on effect is that the longer customers are retained, the greater is the opportunity for cross selling.

In essence, traditional CRM is about making it easier for the customer to deal with you; customers should not have to deal with your complexity, complexity which is often brought about by outdated structures and legacy systems and technologies. The customer should decide how they want to transact business and their preferred channel and not vice versa. Equally, it is about analysing customer information for business decisions: the aim being to help organisations understand customer needs; differentiate between customers via market segmentation; predict likelihood of customer churn; perform analysis of customer loyalty, customer profitability, channel effectiveness and profitability and sales campaign performance. The challenge for an organisation is to move to a situation where the customer starts buying from you rather than being sold to.

Most financial institutions know implicitly that some customers are more profitable than others yet many go on treating all customers in the same way. Many banks have thought that the 80/20 rule applied: i.e. that 80 per cent of profits come from 20 per cent of customers. In fact, some banks have found that highprofit households may in fact represent in excess of 100 per cent of profits because unprofitable ones subtract so much. Through customer profitability analysis, others have found that loyal customers are not necessarily profitable if they were also high users of the companies services.

There is a need to understand the value that present customers— potential long-term value—and potential customers can bring to a financial institution. Failure to take note of customer needs and the understanding that all customers cannot be treated in the same way can only lead to costly investment mistakes. Lenders such as Halifax and Abbey National in the UK have introduced schemes where borrowers can get better rates on their other products if they already have a mortgage. In an expression of its mutuality, Britannia Building Society gives customers a share of its profits each year, based on the size of their borrowing and how long they have been customers. Fidelity investment implements a strategy of differentiated customer relationships, even prioritising and routing telephone calls at call centres on the basis of customer scoring.

E-Trade and other online financial services sites have turned the relationship between banks and customers on its head by empowering the consumer through the provision of real-time information, comparison tools and portfolio-tracking capabilities. Germany's Net.Bank offer customers the ability to tailor-make their own web homepage; customers can retrieve information on about 250,000 stock prices and get news on political affairs, business, sport or cultural events. Banco Santander in Spain informs major credit card users of the status of their accounts as soon as they log-on to its web site. Banks wall increasingly use 'push technology', such as on screen ticker tapes, to inform the customer of new products or relevant account information such as excess cash in a non-interest bearing account.

Viable customer relationships are based on data that have been transformed into actionable information that in turn becomes customer insight ('knowledge') to be used to create predictive models for active customer interaction and actual dialogue it desired. Many financial organisations now use sophisticated profitability, potential and propensity models to determine how best to invest scarce marketing resources.

As marketing moves to a one-to-one environment, the need for large amounts of detailed information about customers is becoming essential. Without customer-level information and data on their transaction behaviour and their likelihood to repurchase and purchase additional products, one-to-one marketing programmes are not possible. Furthermore, as financial institutions begin to understand the profitability of their customers and need to focus resources on retraining, acquiring high profit customers, information on these customers is crucial in the delivery of a successful marketing strategy.

How can a retail bank truly understand and predict its customers' needs to the point where it can design products and services that suit their needs? One way of looking at customers can be from the standpoint of channel usage. In the UK's Lloyds Bank/TSB merger, data were sourced from both their data warehouses, then used to segment the customer base by service channel usage. Customers were allocated to segments on their usage of the following channels: ATMs, automated (direct debits/ standing orders), cards (credit and debit) and telephone.

Australia's St George Bank believed it could raise its conversion rate—i.e. the proportion of initial mortgage inquiries resulting in mortgages—so it tailored its services to match each customer's level of purchasing sophistication. Using a datawarehouse, it categorises prospects as novices, enthusiasts, judicious buyers, investors and the indifferent. This allowed bank staff to respond in a way tailored to the customer, offering the most appropriate level of care and attention. A pilot study showed the conversion rate rising from 33 to 51 per cent, increasing profit while at the same time improving service to customers. Theme-based marketing is being increasingly practiced by financial institutions. The belief is that consumers will no longer shop only for discrete products but for outcomes like a vacation or comfortable retirement. Theme-based marketing can be centred upon general lifestyles such as marriage or buying a home or life goals such as a comfortable retirement. British Airways, offers loans to help people fund their vacations; the Woolwich are offering cars for sale that meet the needs and lifestyles of their customers. It is argued that financial services organisations are ideally positioned for theme-based marketing as they are seen as having the advantage of brand as the trust that derives from the traditional roie as the family fiduciary.

Insurers (such as those in life assurance, personal non-life and health insurance) have tended to hoard extremely detailed records on their customers, claims and costs as islands of data held apart by a product-driven culture, accident, tradition and job protection. Having collected all this data about their customers and potential customers, they have all tended to disregard it as a source of competitive advantage or as a means of reducing cost.

Ironically, the actuarial staffs have built sophisticated models for pricing products and finance teams have spent time building clever costing systems. The marketing teams, however, are only-finding their feet but the most advanced are starting to establish marketing databases with campaign management tools, some modeling and ad hoc query capability.

Union Bank of Norway had the vision to move 'from being one bank into a million banks—one for each customer.' As soon as a customer walks into a branch of UBN he/she is treated like an individual. Customers swipe their bank card through a terminal and are issued with a rather special numbered queuing ticket. This ticket links directly to the banks data warehouse, which instantly identifies the customer and sends a message back to say just who is waiting. From this point on the customer is more than just a number. A video screen above the teller booths shows advertisements tailored to that customer—if the transaction stored in the data warehouse show that the customer has applied for a mortgage, the video screen might run an advert for home insurance.

In a similar vein, Wells Fargo has put in place its first steps toward offering individualised ATM advertising to its customers. It is in effect leasing screen space to third parties. Advertisements appear on the welcome, wait and thank you screens during all ATM transactions. The ads can be changed daily and different ads can be sent to different machines, thus permitting localised advertising. Wells' eventual ambition is to target advertisement messages to customers based on the demographic and financial information the bank maintains in its customer databases.

An increasing number oi companies are using integrated voiced recognition (IVR) and voice recognition systems (VRS) at the customer interface. While this may seem efficient on paper, it often means that callers to a call centre have to endure 3 minutes of music before getting through to a human voice. Many of the calls are ' purchasers-in-waiting.'

Brand loyalty—that emotional connection with customers-is built on the front line—face-to-face, on the phone and over the Internet. For Bank One, the approach is to deliver the right experience when focused on the five customer 'touchpoints', serving the customer with the values of what they call 'I CARE'. I CARE is an Acronym for:

- Inquire: ask questions to identify needs or concerns
- Communicate—assure customers that we are eager to meet their needs
- Affirm: confirm abilities and desires to get the job done
- Recommend—suggest a range of options
- Express: let the customer know we are personally committed.

In short, financial services organisations will want to know who their best customers are, how to keep them and how to increase their 'share of wallet' by knowing what other service or product they can sell to them. They will want to have a customer-centric or one-to-one relationship and to increase shareholder value. But this all boils down to managing customers and potential customers more effectively. To do this you require information that can help make the best decisions to create and manage the right relationships, risks, costs and markets. If financial organisations understand how customers behave and how they prefer to interact, they can redesign core product offerings and devise appropriate channel strategies.

Management of the Total Enterprise

The experience with early CRM forays is that it is imperative to have total front-office/back-office integration. Customer-facing functions such as sales, marketing, call centres and other on-line support must become organisationally integrated with backoffice processes.

Unfortunately, many banks operate as a string of carefully shielded fiefdoms, using individual departments setting up software and systems to handle core function that may or may not interact with other functional areas. For example, account inquiries or automated clearinghouse (ACH) transfers may be processes on one system, stock trades on another, and international transactions on a third. These systems may run on separate mainframes and must be accessed through widely varying interfaces.

Consequently, solutions which have been implemented have been point solutions, aiming at automating only a specific piece of the overall process, disconnected from actions which precede or follow their one specific focus. Each step in the process requires information to be effective, and these systems, built as silos, do not have the ability to leverage shared information. The result is duplicated information, conflicting information, out-of-date information, and in general the inability to get all information needed to all relevant parties when needed. Organisations are increasingly moving from datacentric point solutions to customer-centric enterprise solutions.

The securities industry, for example, is engaged in a massive effort to automate and speed up the process of clearing and settling trades—a concept referred to as straight through processing (STP). The objective is to squeeze the settlement period down from three or more days after trading (T 3) to one (T 1). In many institutions back-office staff often have to deal with 15 per cent or more exceptions—trades that fail to settle smoothly. Usually these trades fail because data is missing or inconsistent, or confirmations do-not arrive or match, or the trades contravene some rules or other. Many institutions have increasingly looked to outsource their back-office operations yet the back-office can be considered as a rich source of information that could be packaged in to a wide variety of high-value services for customers. Equally, it is an information-rich mirror of the entire industry value-chain that the bank could be uniquely positioned to help streamline.

Conclusion

The oft made statement that all economies need a banking system but not necessarily banks is beginning to come to fruition. Many players in today's financial services industry are non-banks and non-financial service organisations; just look at players like Marks & Spencer, AT&T, Intuit, General Motors, Virgin and British Gas Consumer electronics giant Sony have recently announced their intention to provide online financial services through their Dreamcast electronic games consoles.

Today, banks are no longer gatekeepers but gateways to financial products, In the old gatekeeper model, the bank functioned as an inhibiting intermediary that restricted a customer's set of product choices, in the new gateway model, the bank functions as a flexible intermediary that provides access to an entire spectrum of products and delivery channels. Some of the products—insurance, entertainment, travel, investment management—may not even originate from within the bank but instead be provided by third parties. It is possible that banks will be one type of trusted portal, part of peoples' personal connection to e-commerce. And institutions that fail to keep up with the online revolution are likely to find themselves regulated to supplying financial commodities to intermediaries. While IT plays a vital role in CRM happenings, as with ail IT investments it should be driven by a strategic management perspective. Too often, companies seek to build CRM capabilities by designing a powerful IT system without considering wider business issues.

In the e-business world, success is about owning the customers total experience and this is premised on understanding the customer and customer behaviour. Customers expect to interact with an institution through any channel, whatever is convenient for them, and receive instant, high-quality personalised service The customer's experience in transacting business is important and the channel should be aware of the history. Technology should be used to create value for customers.

Integrated information is paramount for successful management of customer relationships. Information is the essential enabler when based on scaleable technology as the platform—that is, information is centrally managed, enterprise-wide and registers as the 'one version of the truth' and provides a consolidated view of the customer across all channels and products.

To manage the transition to a customer centric organisation, organisations must develop the capabilities to acquire the key resources, knowledge, and tools that can help them match customers with appropriate products and services. Unfortunately, many banks have a culture that may be inconsistent with the desire to organise around the customer, and a set of processes that are siloed along product lines instead of customer lines Furthermore, they have a legacy of customers—many of whom are unprofitable— and an inability to properly develop strategies that will give all segments of the customer base the service that suits them.

Traditional financial service companies also struggle with the cultural, organisational and technological challenges associated with becoming customer focused enterprises. The sheer size and historical baggage of traditional financial institutions can have a negative implication in the new ecology. In many banks, the branch is the central point of reference: accounts are held there.

It is very likely, that in the future banks will need to use their distribution networks to sell non-financial products if they are to remain competitive. In the UK there have already been examples of successful collaborations between financial and non-financial organisations. Barclaycard and Cellnet, for example, offered customers cellular telephones linked to Barclays' loyalty scheme, Barclaycard has also partnered gas utility Eastern and the Ford Motor Company.

Speed is of the essence when competing in the new ecology and this has implications for the IT function. WingspanBank was established by Bank One in a very short timescale. In January 1999, a small team was charged with building a full-service online bank. By February, the group was ready to build the bank. They met with vendors to finalise hardware and software choices and simultaneously put the company together. The team started development immediately, testing was completed in April and went live in June.

Technology and the new economy offer tremendous opportunities for existing bricks-and-mortar organisations. There are lots of opportunities; and the ecosystem is being continually defined and refined. There is, however, the danger that the organisation neglects the basics. Competing in the marketspace does not mean that the past is irrelevant. Many of the attributes that made organisations successful in the past are still crucial. Organisations still require strong leadership; the right structures and processes must be put in place; the right people with the right skills, attitudes and competencies hired and deployed appropriately; technology must become part of management 'theory of business'. All must be incorporated within a sound strategic business perspective.

The case of Bank One is worth recounting. Despite being an internel pioneer with its online bank WingspanBank.com the institution has had some problems recently. In an interview in early 1999 the CEO staled 'someone asked mo what causes me to wake up in the middle ot the night 11 used to be bad loans. I don't work about bad loans any more'. He confessed that he worries about the Internet. In October later that year he lost out in a bank shakeout brought about by the poor performance of its credit and division due to bad loans! He eventually resigned in December

HOTEL RESERVATION: GIVING THE LOWEST PRICE GUARANTEE

The increase in the volume of online bookings through the internet has had a major impact on both distribution channels and profitability in the hotel industry. According to the consulting firm Forrester Research, sales of online leisure hotel rooms doubled in 2002 to $2.7 billion. Research indicates that one in three hotel rooms will be booked online by 2006, up from less than one in ten in 2002. While this growth of internet bookings has driven up the profits and market values of internet travel agencies, the increasing use of the internet by consumers has not necessarily had a similar positive impact on profitability for the lodging industry. The proliferation of internet travel agencies suggests that such firms provide a much needed market intermediation function that the lodging industry does not provide—and that the profits currently enjoyed by these agencies represent a leakage of potential profits that could be reclaimed by the lodging industry. This growing trend may be, in part, fueled by consumers who increasingly view hotel room services as homogeneous within given segments, with rooms from one brand serving as a near perfect substitute for rooms from another. This indifference results in consumers choosing their hotels based on the lowest rates available and is facilitated by searching among the various distribution channels. Not surprisingly, third party internet travel website companies, such as Expedia, Orbitz, and Travelocity, have become extremely popular largely due to their ability to facilitate the consumer with a low-cost search. By making it easier and less "time costly" to compare room rates between different hotels, these online travel service companies have empowered the consumer with the information to comparison shop for rooms given a stated quality and rate preference. This further complicates the competitive dynamics since some of the inventory of rooms available for sales by internet online travel service (OTS) companies are provided by an individual hotel owners or hotel operators to third-party consolidators. Individual hotel owners and operators often release large blocks of rooms for sale through internet travel agencies such as Travelocity at deep discounts during slow periods. As they feel this action is a mechanism of boosting room revenue and selling rooms that could often go unsold. These rooms are often sold in the aftermarket at prices that undercut those of rooms offered for sale by the brand's own website. The pricing and discounting of these rooms is accomplished through what is known as the merchant model, whereby internet travel companies are assigned blocks of rooms at far below standard current market rates and then resold over the internet at significant mark-ups. Extensive use of third party internet bookings under the merchant model has resulted in the erosion of the unified pricing plans that are favoured by the brand-name hotel companies. It is reasonable to anticipate that as the practice of shopping for rooms on the Internet becomes more widely accepted, hotel companies will continue to battle for control and market influence over their pricing structure, inventory of rooms, and their ability to foster brand loyalty. The loss of control over pricing of rooms within a brand and the potential transfer of pricing authority to third-party OTS companies stem from the consumers' desire to obtain the lowest rate within their desired market segment. From the perspective of the consumer, room rates offered by comparable brands within a competitive set are uncertain and unknown at the actual time the reservations are made. Therefore, when making the initial reservation the consumer will often choose to visit the various distribution channels, including the hotel's own website, seeking the lowest rate for hotels within their chosen segment and location. Furthermore, because rates often change prior to their reservation arrival date, consumers face uncertainty in rates over time even for the same hotel in a given market. As a result of these combined forces, consumers will often continue to search after having made their reservation in hopes of identifying a lower priced hotel room that represents, in their own mind, a reasonable substitute to the room already booked. If one is located prior to the cancellation deadline the customer will cancel the initial reservation and re-book at the lower rate. The combination of increased downward price pressure from third-party OTS companies and the post-reservation search and switch behaviour of consumers will by definition have a significant impact on hotel profitability and pricing. It may be attractive for hotel companies to believe they can regain control over the pricing process though improved brand differentiation, tighter standards on inventory and partnering with other companies to form distribution alliances. However, the strong incentive of consumers to search for and book rooms at the lowest price suggest that another potential solution to this problems lies with dealing with the consumers' incentive to search. This solution has the capacity to eliminate the need for consumers to search for lower rates, and therefore increase retention of the brand's customer base and relies on eliminating the price uncertainty they face when making a reservation. If this uncertainty can resolved at the time of the initial reservation, there will be no incentive for consumers to seek lower rates from third party online distributors' channels.

We propose that, by providing alternative forms of reservations, any hotel can effectively eliminate the incentive of the guest to search and therefore eliminate the probability that the consumer will cancel their reservation and switch to a comparable room at a different hotel or even an identical room in the same hotel. Our model builds on the work of Quan (2002) who showed that a hotel reservation can be compared to a financial European Call Option given by the hotel to the guest—that is, the guest has the right but not the obligation (since they can cancel costlessly, within the cancellation period) to purchase the services of a hotel room at a specific date in the future at the set reservation price. When used as a call option, the guest can "lock-in" the minimum rate they will pay for a room; that is, if rates increase, they can hold the reservation and pay the reserved-room price, but if the rate decreases they can cancel the reservation and rebook at the lower rate. A key insight from Quan's work is that a reservation given by a hotel is valued by the customer (and costly to the hotel) since it commits the hotel to sell at a fixed price when the actual rates on a given day are uncertain to both the customer and the hotel.

Thus, one needs to expand upon this concept and propose an "exotic" reservation to address the hotel industry's immediate concern as described in our opening—the migration of customers to third-party OTS companies and the subsequent search and switch behaviour of consumers continuing to seek lower room rates. As a solution we propose guaranteed lowest-price reservation which is analogous to a "look-back" call option. A look-back call option allows the option holder to purchase an item at the lowest traded price for the item over the length of the option contract. In this type of exotic reservation, the guest is guaranteed to pay the lowest price offered and booked at the hotel distribution channel employed throughout the period of the reservation. We determine the value of this guarantee and in so doing determine the price that the hotel should charge for this guarantee. By providing the guest with the assurance they will pay the lowest rate offered to transient guests on a given day, there will be no incentive for them to search elsewhere, thereby eliminating the deleterious affects of search and switch behaviour on hotel profits while simultaneously allowing hotel companies to reassert control over the pricing of their rooms. Furthermore, we use the model determine the value of existing low price guarantees presently offered by many hotel companies. It is found that such guarantees in their present form have little value to the consumer and therefore do not provide the price guarantee feature that our proposed "exotic" reservation provides.

Post-Reservation 'Search and Switch" Behaviour

In response to their desire to regain more control over their brands pricing, hotel companies have devised mechanisms to both circumvent internet travel agents and provide disincentives to booking rooms on these sites. One such example is Travelweb.com, a site owned by Dallas based Pegasus with partners Hilton Hotels, Hyatt, Marriott International, Intercontinental Hotels Group, Starwood Hotels and Resorts and Priceline. com. This partnership is designed to circumvent the need to use internet travel sites, created as an internet travel agent, but one that is owned by the hotel partners themselves and one where the maximum mark-up within the merchant model is limited to 15 to 20 per cent. In theory, owners of hotels associated with the brand partners would engage Travelweb.com to sell their excess inventory but the erosion of prices would be controlled due to the limit on mark-ups by the reseller. Presumably this would provide an incentive to hotels to sell their excess inventory to Travelweb, as a larger share of the room revenue would stay with the hotel itself. However, the ability to control price discounting in this manner is dependent upon the proportion of the total rooms controlled by the partners in any one market. If there are a large number of rooms controlled by other brands and independent hotels that are not part of the 'cartel' created by the partnership in Travelweb and if these competitor hotels release lower priced rooms to consumers through other internet travel agents like Travelocity, who in turn sell them at lower prices than comparable hotel rooms that are sold on Travelweb, then the hotel companies in Travelweb will be forced to meet these lower prices or surrender market share. Another mechanism being used to regain control over consumer hotel booking behaviour is limiting frequent travel points to those rooms booked over the company's own website or over other approved vendors. Hilton Hotels, for instance no longer offers HHonors points and mileage to people who booked rooms on bargain websites. This is designed to provide a clear disincentive to customers seeking to find lower prices on discount online travel agents by denying any frequent traveller points for that stay. This incentive will only work up to the point where consumers value the marginal miles earned by that stay more than the amount saved per room night by booking on the discount online travel agent. Since the rooms over these sites often save customers from $10 to $40 or more per night, the value of the frequent traveller points lost will often be far less than the amount saved. Of course, in those cases where the discount agents' and the hotels own site's prices are essentially identical, this will provide some, marginal incentive for customers to book rooms through the company's own website.

 A different approach to controlling the flow of guests who make their reservations through internet travel discounters has been introduced by hotel companies such as Cendant, Intercontinental Hotels Group and Starwood. These companies have instituted 'lowest price guarantees' on reservations made through the company's online booking services. These programmes offer the assurance that; if after a guest has booked a room using the hotel's brand website, the guest finds a lower rate for the same room on the same day at the same hotel sold on any online distributor website, the company will match the lower rate. Most programmes even offer an additional percentage discount on the match price, say 10 per cent, if a lower rate is found. The Best Price Guarantee programme offered by Cendant provides an example. The Cendant Best Price Guarantee promises that if customers find lower published rates for their hotels through any other online distributor, Cendant will match the lower rate plus an additional 10 per cent discount. The customer must first book a reservation using the brand website. If within a 24 hour period from the time of booking the customer finds a lower rate online, they must submit the lower rate via an e-mail to their customers service department who much then verify the information. If verified, customer service will provide the matched rate plus a 10 per cent discount reservation. Such programmes attempt to provide consumers with the assurance that the rates offered at brand websites are the lowest available, and therefore there is no need to shop for lower rates at other online booking sites. The availability of rooms offered by third-party internet sellers is largely determined by the willingness of franchisees to sell their rooms to these providers. To discourage such activities, the hotel companies often make the case that by participating in such Best Price Guarantees programmes, franchisees can earn a higher room yield than if they had sold their rooms. The benefit to the franchisee of participating in this programme comes from the observation that the franchisee's room revenue from the matching price and the discount is higher than if they had sold the room to third party sellers. This is due to the higher mark-up that third-party sellers require with the so-called merchant model as compared to the resulting mark-up from selling a room at the Best Price Guarantee. For example, assume a room is sold to the wholesaler for $100. Given that the usual wholesaler mark-up is 20 per cent, the wholesale would sell this room at their website for $120. If the room is sold by the wholesaler, the hotel realizes a yield of $100 for the room.

It is often pointed out by the parent hotel company that with the price matching programme, the hotel will be better-off to not sell their rooms to the wholesalers. So long as the mark-up for the wholesaler is higher than that of the hotel, the price guarantee reservation will always be able to undercut the wholesaler and retain a higher yield for the rooms. Although such programmes appear to give the guest the assurance that by booking at the brand's website they would be assured of the lowest rate, in actuality, the 24 hour time limit from the day of the reservation makes this guarantee essentially worthless. A more valuable and realistic best-rate guarantee can be developed and priced whereby the hotel can offer a rate that is guaranteed to be the best rate that a consumer will ever be able to find for that room (or a comparable room) from the date of the reservation until the date of arrival. In effect, the company would be eliminating the consumer's incentive to search the web tor cheaper room rates as the arrival date-approaches. Experience tells us thai, as the arrival date approaches, if there often significant unsold inventory, when such unsold room inventing exists, this will trigger larger amounts of rooms being released to discount online travel sites and provide a growing-population of more deeply discounted rooms being made available on the internet. Any "best rate guarantee" that does not take into consideration the shopping behaviour of consumers and discounting behaviour of sellers cannot be of much value in the market to either the consumer nor will it be effective at addressing the underlying need of hotel companies to control customer migration following search and switch activities.

Reservation Guarantee—Conceptual Issues

The present problem facing the hotel industry as a result of internet shopping is basically similar to a problem that has been well explored in the economics literature in broad area of information economics. In the context of hotels, there is information asymmetry between the hotel operator and the guest. The guests have diverse private information and preferences as to their rationale to purchase a room at a specific hotel. Different guests may be motivated by different hotel attributes, these include among others, brand loyalty, the location of the hotel, the service the hotel offers, and of course, the price paid. If the hotel could perfectly observe each guest's set of preferences in all dimensions, they would then be able to price discriminate and charge a different room rate based on each consumer's willingness to pay. An example of this practice is the pricing of higher room rates for weekdays, when price insensitive business travellers book their rooms, and discounting during the weekend, when leisure travellers often book. However, from the hotel operator's perspective, they do not generally explicitly observe such differences when they set their reservation booking policies. Thus it is not surprising that no single policy will be suitable for all customers given the diverse nature of their tastes and preferences. To achieve a closer correspondence between the rate charged and the consumer's willingness to pay, it is reasonable to explore the possibility of offering alternative reservations in the hopes that they serve the customers better and at the same time increase the customers' interest in staying at the hotel. Our suggested solution to resolving this issue is to offer a menu of different types of reservations and have the customers self-select and thereby provide a better match between the needs of the guest and the hotel operator. In implementing the specific reservation model presented here, we target one dimension of a room booking that OTS companies emphasize— room rates. By offering a modified reservation with an option, those guests who are most sensitive to price uncertainty will choose to select the "exotic" reservation while those who are less sensitive and those who have a strong brand loyalty, will select the more standard method of booking as a lower price offered in the future at a competing property would not motivate them to switch their reservation to the other property. Therefore, our model does not ignore brand loyalty—the group that values brand loyalty above any price differential is still being served by the normal reservation process. However, guests who have migrated to third party websites and engaged in search and switch behaviour would find the "exotic" reservations format attractive.

In broad terms, our proposed reservation model takes into explicit consideration differences in the preferences of hotel guests and their heterogeneous valuation of room services. Customers chose hotel rooms for a variety of reasons, including brand loyalty, location, service, and, of course, price. By introducing our proposed reservation format, concurrent with conventional forms of reservations, we specifically target those customers whose room decisions are motivated primarily by price rather than by brand or another attribute specific to the hotel. This is achieved by designing a set of terms in our proposed reservation formats such that price sensitive customers, the same ones who use OTS companies to shop for the lowest price regardless of brand, will find it to their best interest to self-select and therefore willingly adopt our proposed reservation terms. For those guests whose booking practices are largely driven by brand (or other reasons), our alternative reservation option (given its cost) will be less appealling and therefore these consumers will likely find conventional room reservations acceptable. The requirement that both (or possibly more) forms of reservations should be offered concurrently is an explicit recognition that guests have heterogeneous tastes and preferences and that although brand may be extremely important to a certain segment of guests, our approach only targets those who are less driven by brand but by obtaining the best price with the use of the internet.

The Low Price Guarantee Model

The Low Price Guarantee Model would work as follows: A guest makes a reservation for a room at price R at $t = 0$ for a $t = T$ check-in. The hotel guarantees that the price the guest will pay at $t = T$ will be the lowest web-published price for the room from $t = 0$ until check-in, if the lowest web price is less than R, If the lowest price over this period is above R, the guest will pay R, the rate promised by the reservation for the room.

Thus a guest, in the absence of this low-price guarantee, will pay R at check-in for the room. At the time of booking, the future web-published prices are unknown and may change for a variety of reasons. Although there is future price uncertainty, the guest, by making a reservation, has essentially locked in a price R for the room and therefore has eliminated any price uncertainty.

Define the lowest web price over the period $t = 0, T$ as P_{min}. That is,

$$P_{min} = min\ (P_0, P_1, P_2, P ..., P_T)$$

By accepting the low-price guarantee, the benefit to the guest is the difference between R and if P_{min} if $R > P_{min}$. Alternatively, if $P_{min} > R$ over the entire period, the low-price guarantee does not yield a payoff since the guest will pay R, the price the guest would have paid in the absence of this guarantee. Thus the payoff for the guest from receiving this guarantee is:

This payoff structure is identical to the payoff to the holder of a put option—that is, the owner of the option has the right but not the obligation to sell the room back to the hotel at R, the reserved rate. Thus the guest will only do so if the price of the room to the guest is lower than R.

Conceptually, this option gives the guest the right (but not the obligation) to sell the room back to the hotel at R, the reservation price, for P_{min}. Clearly this will only be P_{min} profitable if $P_{min} < R$. Thus the guest will only do so if the minimum price experienced is lower than the reservation price. Note that this is the same payoff as if the guest exercises the put option optimally.

This is sometimes called a put option on Extrema (Conze and Viswanathan, 1991) since the condition of the payoff is dependent on an extreme value (in this case, the minimum price achieved). Conze and Viswanathan showed that for the case $R < P_0$ the value of this option is:

where

and N(o) represents the normal distribution function, o represents the volatility of prices and is a measure of the price uncertainty over future T periods.

A low price guarantee has value because it offers the guest protection against uncertainty in future room rates provided by competing hotels. Since it is this uncertainty that drives our model, it is important to understand how it is characterized and how it relates to more familiar existing yield management practices that attempt to take such factors into consideration. Our model of hotel room price uncertainty parallels closely those developed in the financial options-pricing literature. An option is viewed as a contingent claim on an asset whose future returns are uncertain. Since the option's payoff is contingent on the asset's future return, the option's value today is a function of the probability of having a positive payoff in the future. This probability is determined by the specification of a stochastic process which characterizes the distribution of future returns, Thus uncertainty is modelled as a stochastic process which provides a probabilistic characterization of future returns. The overall return process is viewed as being comprised of a deterministic predictable component, or drift term, and an unpredictable stochastic component, Because an option is a claim on some unknown future value of the asset, its value is dependent on the stochastic component oi returns and not on the drift term. Thus in the calibration of option pricing models, whereby uncertainty is measured as the volatility of the stochastic component, the uncertainty is often measured as the standard deviation of returns after returns have been purged of all predictable movements. In our hotel reservation application, we analogously envision hotel room prices movements over time as being comprised of these two components. In the context of hotel room rates, reasonable measures of predictable price movements are those that are forecasted by conventional yield management models. One function of yield management is to predict future room occupancies or rates using a variety of forecasting models, ranging from time series models such as exponential smoothing and AR1MA models to advanced additive and multiplicative booking models (Kimes and Weatherford, 2003), Other predictable elements taken into consideration may include seasonal factors and holidays. In this area, great attention is given to predicting the future demand for rooms and the prices that should be charged. Thus predictions from such models represent the best estimates of the future and therefore capture all the predictable movement in future prices or room occupancies. Given this interpretation, the stochastic component can be simply viewed as the forecast errors or the residuals from the application of yield management models. Thus a reasonable estimate of uncertainty or volatility is the standard deviation of the error term in yield management forecasts. Since the value of our low price guarantee reservation is dependent on the size of the unpredictable component, it is important to get an indication as to its magnitude. Due to the wide use of yield management practices, there have been numerous studies which have attempted to quantify their accuracy. In a study comparing the forecast performance of regression, pick-up and multiplicative models, the mean absolute percentage error (MAPE) of forecasts ranged from 10 per cent for the pick-up and regression models to over 200 per cent for the multiplicative model (Kimes and Weatherford, 2003). In another study of group bookings, the MAPE ranged from 10-15 per cent on the day of arrival to 40 per cent at two months before arrival (Kimes, 1999). Both these results indicate that although yield management practices do have some reasonable forecasting ability, a substantial amount of future changes in room demand is unpredictable.

Hospitality Software, Reservation, Property and Revenue Management Solutions

Major Areas of Operation:
- Property Management Software
- Online Booking Solutions
- Marketing Services
- We Generate Bookings for Yon
- Improving the Efficiency of your Business
- Increasing Revenue
- Reducing Costs
- Improving your Customer Service

All our products are multi-lingual, multi-currency and compliant with Sales Tax regimes all over the world. Designed to be scalable for use in single user or networked environments. Suitable for all property types villas, apartments, hotels, hostels, motels, yachts, boats or any other accommodation type billed on a nightly basis,

Experienced Management Team

- Over 50 years of travel and hospitality industry experience
  - Providing Software Systems and Internet Services
  - Running Hotels and International Travel Companies
  - Running Self Catering accommodation, Villas and Cottages
- Over 50 years of Software Industry experience
  - Building brands
  - Developing high quality successful software products
  - Selling products and services globally

"We know what we are doing"

A Few USP's

- Guests receive an invoice in their language
- You can book more than accommodation using our online facility. Transfers, Entertainment, insurance. Bike hire or anything else you want to offer at the time of hooking
- Invoices in the guest currency and yours
- Add a display screen with guest welcome messages and other information in your reception area
- Built in support for agencies
- Corporate/Promotional discounts or offers
- No annual support contracts
- Integrated backup and recovery process
- We will help you generate bookings from the internet
- The same product can support multiple property and accommodation types
- Scaleable. Priced in accordance to the size of your property

A Fresh Approach

Our products are multi-lingual and multi-currency and Sales Tax compliant worldwide. This enables us to build a global business and not one restricted to one market sector or country. Our global approach enables great features to be added to our products to improve your customer service. Our hospitality and travel experience help us add functionality which are relevant to property owners and the global travel market.

The Benefits to You

- Easy to use products delivering the functionality you require at a price you can justify
- Increased customer services to your guests
- We are aware of global trends and develop our products accordingly
- Unique software features
- For multi-country operations—one product solution, reduced training and other benfits
- Meet the needs of international guests in ways your competitors cannot

Internet

We have been developing Internet solutions since 1997. Our products are designed with the future in mind. *Our* skills cover Search Engines, websites and using them to generate bookings. The Internet is fully integrated to our products and not tagged on "the end." We will show you how to use our products to generate bookings and other revenue which can cover the investment in our products

Support

The founders have built global software businesses before Software developed for sale globally must be technically perfect, otherwise support is difficult and expensive. Therefore our products are developed with this in mind.

Accommres has been over 2 years in the making. Our first live site was in Spain, July 2003. They and other sites have ironed out technical and other issues so that you and we can be confident that we can deliver our products and service anywhere.

We do not believe in charging you to fix our bugs (the rest of the software industry does)

- No annual support contract charges
- Free software updates

AccommRes Property Management Solutions

The answer is yes. Whether your needs are sophisticated or not AccommRes covers it all. Invoices in your customers language, Group bookings, Integration to devices in the property. Management reports keep you in control. Move people from room to room with the click of a mouse. Look at room allocations or bookings in your property on one screen. Easy to use and configurable. If you only have a villa you do not need to check guests in or out, AccommRes gives you this felixibility. Invoice and enter payments in over 40 currencies. Check in forms, vehicle information and even the ability to scan passport or other ID documents. Unlimited "extras" can be billed to bookings. We even include easy to use Backup and Restore facilities.

The professional edition is ideal for use in multi-room or multi-unit properties or travel companies who need to do more than just book a room.

AccommRes Online Booking Solutions

The answer is yes. AccommRes builds your online booking site in multiple languages. We provide all the internet resources. The site is configured from information entered in AccommRes. Pictures are included. Importantly your booking site is fully syncronised to the AccommRes property management module. You do not need to login to separate online systems to manually update availability and pricing information and then manually update bookings to the PMS. Unique features such as supporting agents, corporate offers and the ability to book more than accommodation are included. Add a range of definable extras to the booking form for example Travel Insurance, Transfers, Entertainment, the list is endless. All you need is a PC and an internet connection.

AccommRes will turn your website into a 24 hour booking site answering enquiries, checking availability, generating prices and taking bookings.

RSI INTERNATIONAL INC: A CASE STUDY

RSI International is a world-leader in web-based reservation and property management systems with integrated real-time room reservation capabilities. By increasing revenue and reducing expenses, our products have proven time and time again that they boost the profitability of our hotel and resort industry customers.

Key benefits of our systems and model:

- Cost efficiency
- "AnyTime Any Where" access
- Short lead time to deployment
- End to End solution provider

Whether you are looking for your first system, or to upgrade an existing one, RSI offers specialized, web-based, property management and reservation solutions suited to your needs.

- InnQuick™: Property management systems for full service properties with 50 rooms or less.
- HotelSoft$_{IM}$; Properly management systems for full service properties with 50 rooms or more,
- PropSoft™: A fully integrated suite of solution includes our InnQuick or HotelSoft property management systems and Home Owner Accounting (HOA) designed specifically to manage individually owned but centrally controlled and operated properties.

- ResLinxII™: Web-based reservation booking .systems that adds e-reservation capabilities to all RSI Property Management Systems and your current services.
- OneRez™: Web-based Central Reservation System (CRS) tor multi-properties inventory for call centre and e-reservation functionalities.
- HOA—Home Owner Accounting: A stand alone accounting programme for individually owned, but centrally controlled and operated properties.
- Web-Based Systems: Our product line is web-based meaning that you access the applications on the RSI hosted server using high-speed Internet connections.

Products Web-Based Systems

Our product line is web-based meaning that you access the applications on the RSI hosted server using high-speed Internet connections. Your e-reservations can still be accepted and processed if for any reason your property is disconnected from the server.

Your data is all stored on our server and RSI takes total responsibility for security and backup. This data, however, remains your property entirely and can be downloaded by you when required.

Benefits of RSI's web-based systems

Live Online Bookings

RSI's web-based systems enable live online availability and booking. These e-reservations can be automatically processed in real-time basis eliminating the risk of double bookings.

Implementing Change Much Simpler

When you need to adapt to evolving business needs, our web-based system makes change and upgrading a far simpler task than the on-site server model. RSI does the necessary work for you at our end without even visiting your property.

Reduces Cost of Ownership

As your applications are running on our remote server, any PC with an Internet connection will allow you access to our server you do not need to purchase new and expensive hardware.

Lowers Maintenance Costs

RSI takes care of maintaining the lull functionality of applications reducing or eliminating the need for you to employ your own IT experts.

Secure Data Backup

RSI provides a full backup service ensuring no data is irretrievably lost.

Connectivity between Multiple Properties

Each property in a chain can check real time availability online, share data, and even take bookings for each other.

Global Remote Access

You or your staff can access your system from anywhere in the world for instant information on business activity.

Reduces the Damage of Hardware Failure

If your hardware should fail drastically, simply replace your PC and reconnect to our server to be up and running again. No need to reinstall software, reconfigure or download backup data.

What You Need for Connectivity

At the Property

We run an 'application client' at the property with all processing done on the hosted site. Depending upon your requirements, a number of application-layers can be linked' to provide a complete system either for an individual property or hotel chain. These layers are:

- Reservation management layer
- Internet based e-reservation layer
- Property management application layer

To connect from outside of the 'fixed points' of connected PC's, a user can simply plug a laptop into any comm.-line and sign-on using the previously loaded client. This gives your mobile management teams anywhere, any time connectivity.

Environment

- The application client can be run on a standard PC (or a PC-Network or server-centric).
- The application is SQL based.
- Identical software is run on all of the clients.
- New releases are downloaded from the Internet, a process that takes only minutes.

Benefits

- Low hardware/software investment at the property level.
- Low maintenance costs at the property level.
- Any WhereAnyTime™ access to property information.
- All available rooms can be sold to the property and Internet clients.

ASP Model Compared to on-site Server Model Business

Business Question	ASP model	Stand-Alone Model
Where does the application run?	Application server in specialized professional managed server farm environment.	Computer provided by the property.
Where is my data stored?	Database server in specialized professional managed server farm environment, with the option of copying to your property at any time.	Stored on computer at your property. Additional copies are the responsibility of the client.
Backups?	Daily backup with off site secured storage.	Performed by user, extra-cost software and hardware may be required.

Internet Connection Required?	Yes. reservations, updates, and support.	Recommended for

Business Question	ASP model	Stand-Alone Model
Extra Licenses Required? access licenses	None 2000, SQL, client	Microsoft Windows
128-bit encryption security?	Yes	No
Ability to add new functions and updates?	Yes, applied by RSI engineers at no additional charge	Yes, distributed by Internet or CD, hotel responsible for technician to install and configure

- Research, write, edit and translate promotional and informational material (newsletters, conference programmes, corporate brochures, news releases, backgrounders and fact sheets)
- Prepare, organize, research and script presentations including speaker notes, visuals and handout material
- Develop surveys, analyse responses and report on results
- Translate documentation (English to French, French to English), as well as proofread and edit in both official languages

Web/Graphic Design/Pre-Press Production

- Develop comprehensive 'corporate identity' packages for events and clients
- Provide pre-press production services, including design and layout, for the production of print and visual material:
  - Provide camera-ready copy or press-ready film
  - Coordinate printing and document distribution

    ❝ Design and create worldwide web home pages

    ❝ Manage the design and production of regular publications.

Public Relations Projects Support

- Develop communication, business, marketing or action plans
- Coordinate media briefings, news conferences, telephone and video conference calls
- Implement government relations strategies

EXPOMARKETING GROUP: A CASE STUDY

The ExpoMarketing team will make your job simple with our extensive trade show management services. We prepare budgets and timeline for each trade show and track them through our planning process. We work with your existing exhibit house or we will find you the perfect rental exhibit. Floor plan preparation, electrical drawing submission and construction are all part of our trade show services.

ExpoMarketing orders all show services, sets up transportation and labour vendors and even supervise the setup of your trade show display onsite. We know how to order trade show services with cost efficiency in mind. As a trade show management company that offers all the services you will need, you will benefit from having to deal with just one vendor, one check, no mark tips on any show services such as drayage or labour, and you can take advantage of our buying power through our vendor discounts.

Why ExpoMarketing:

- More free time for other activities
- Cost-effective for tight budgets
- No mark-up on show services
- Extensive inventory of rental exhibits
- Graphic design and production in-house
- Promotional campaigns that get results

USU EXTENSION: A CASE STUDY

Our experienced staff and custom software excel in trade show and convention management.

- Design, develop and manage exhibitions and vendor related shows

- Provide custom computer system to manage exhibitor and trade show registration and booth assignments
- Online registration procedures and database management
- Online interactive booth availability and assignment
- Name badge bar-coding technology
- Select and interface with display companies
- Produce comprehensive exhibitor kits
- Onsite staffing and management

ROOM SELLING TECHNIQUES

UPSELLING AT THE FRONT DESK

DEFINTION

Up-selling can be defined as a process of selling a higher priced commodity to a guest than that a guest had actually requested for. E.g. A front office assistant sells a suite room to a guest who had originally requested for a double room.

BRIEF DESCRIPTION

- Up-selling is a very important selling tool used by the hospitality industry sectors across the world.
- In hotels, all the revenue generating departments try to up-sell products such as accommodation product, food and beverage products and a large number of other products and services.
- Up-selling is also used widely by the front office department employees in order to get more business from the guests by recommending them to purchase a higher priced commodity.
- At front desk it is easier to up-sell to a guest coming to the hotel without any reservation.
- The receptionist should have a proper physical appearance and excellent grooming in order to create a good impression on the newly arrived guest.
- The front desk assistant should also have a very good communication skill in order to talk fluently with the guest.

- The front desk assistant should greet the guest warmly and explain the various categories of guestrooms available in the property and should highlight the expensive categories of rooms such as suites to the guests with their features.
- Thus, the front desk assistant should be able to understand the need of the guest and provide him with the best type of room available and at the same time maximize the business for the hotel.

BENEFITS OF UP-SELLING

- Up-selling increases the revenue of the hotel and thus also increases the profit of the hotel.
- Up-selling enables the guests to purchase a better quality product and thus gives them an opportunity to experience and use the better quality product.
- Up-selling benefits the employees also as the front desk assistants are given rewards on the amount of up-selling they do to generate for the hotel.

DISCOUNTS

DEFINITION

Discounts can be defined as price reduction which is offered to the guest by the hotel on various products such as rooms and food and beverage service and other accessory products and services.

THE MAIN REASONS OF OFFERING DISCOUNTS

1. TO REDUCE THE IMPACT OF OFF SEASON

- Discounts play a major role in reducing the impact of off or low season which many hotels face.
- Discounts assure the hotel some business by attracting guests during off season.

2. TO SELL HIGH PRICED AND SLOW MOVING PRODUCTS SUCH AS SUITES

- Discounts help in the sale of high-priced products such as suites in hotels which are not sold very frequently and so come in the category of slow moving products.

3. TO BUILD A GOOD RELATIONSHIP WITH THE GUEST
   - Discounts help in establishing a good relationship with the guest as price-sensitive guests are attracted by this strategy of the hotel.
4. TO BUILD REPEAT BUSINESS WITH THE GUEST
   - Discounts help in generating repeat business for the hotel by attracting the guests again for the next time to come and stay with the hotel and in this way, generates revenue for the hotel.
5. TO COMPETE WITH THE OTHER PALYERS IN THE MARKET
   - Discounts help in keeping the prices of all the hotels in a particular market in a control manner.
   - Thus, discounts help in increase in competition with the various players and thus help a hotel to beat its competitors and be market leader.

BENEFITS TO A HOTEL FOR PROVIDING DISCOUNTS TO ITS GUESTS

1. INCREASE IN CUSTOMER LOYALTY OF THE HOTEL
2. INCREASE IN SALE OF THE SLOW MOVING AND EXPENSIVE PRODUCTS
3. INCREASE IN SALE DURING THE PERIOD OF OFF SEASON
4. INCREASE IN THE OVERALL REVENUE GENERATION AND PROFIT OF A HOTEL
5. INCREASE IN POPULARITY AND GAINING THE POSITION OF A MARKET LEADER

SALES: AN INTRODUCTION

Sales, or the activity of selling, forms an integral part of commercial activity. Mastering sales is considered by many as some sort of persuading "art". On the contrary, the methodological approach of selling refers to it as a systematic process of repetitive and measurable milestones, by which a salesperson relate his offering enabling the buyer to visualize how to achieve his goal in an economic way. Selling is a practical implementation of marketing; it often forms a separate grouping in a corporate structure, employing separate specialist operatives known as salesmen (singular: salesman or salesperson). The successful questioning to understand a customers goal, the further creation of a valuable solution by communicating the necessary information that encourages a buyer to achieve his goal at an economic cost is the responsibility of the sales person or the sales engine (e.g. internet, vending machine, etc). The primary function of professional sales is to generate and close leads, educate prospects, fill needs and satisfy wants of consumers appropriately, and therefore turn prospective customers into actual ones. From a marketing point of view, selling is one of the methods of promotion used by marketers. Other promotional techniques include advertising, sales promotion, publicity, and public relations. Various sales strategies exist, such as tit-for-tat which is best if ongoing dealings and interactions are expected. This insight is behind so-called consultative sales process which are used by Saturn to sell cars, as well as for some direct Business-to-Business sales. Several types of sales exist including direct, consultative, and complex sales, Complex sales varies from other types in that the customer plays a more pro-active role, often requiring proposal response to their Request for Proposal (RFP).

- Modes of selling include:
    - Direct Sales-involving face-to-fare contact
    - Retail or consumer
    - Door-to-door or travelling salesman
    - Business-to-business
- Indirect-human-mediated but with indirect contact
    - Telemarketing or telesales
    - Mail-order
- Electronic
    - Web B2B, B2C
    - EDI
- Agency-based
    - Consignment
    - Multi-level marketing
    - Sales agents (real estate, manufacturing)

Types of sales include:
- Direct sales
- Consultative sales
- Complex sales

In theory, the purpose of selling is to help a customer realize his or her goals in an economic fashion. However, in reality this is not always the case. Customers can be influenced to purchase a product or service that initially was not of interest to them. Some salespeople are trained in the art of selling customers things they do not need. Take for example the purchasing of a car: a consumer may have a set of cars in mind (called an evoked set) that she feels match her needs, wants and budget. She may seek the advice of a salesperson given that a salesperson can help her realize the right car given those criteria. This can be a socially useful function; salespeople have specialized knowledge of products that can help consumers make an informed decision. However, a salesperson may also talk a consumer into purchasing a more expensive or perhaps larger car then she needs or can afford. In this context, the salesperson may have usefully helped the customer re-evaluate her needs, thereby establishing a new set of appropriate choices among which included the newer or large car. This again would be a helpful and useful service provided by the salesperson. However, it is sometimes the case that customers purchase a product or service that was not initially intended and remains an inappropriate purchase after the fact. On the other hand, the consumer in this scenario can be held partially responsible ior the inappropriate purchase; indeed, "A fool and his money are soon parted." This dysfunctional behaviour is encouraged by:

- Incentives of salespeople to increase their total number of sales, especially where retailers keep track of sales or offer commission-based salaries
- Incentives from the manufactures of products or the companies of service providers to salespeople to sell their products where other similar products ottered by competitors are offered
- The incentive to sell a customer a product that is in need of being cleared out, despite the fact that a customer may be better to wait for the new product.

MARKETING: AN INTRODUCTION

Traditionally, marketing has been a term applied to the process or act of bringing together buyers and sellers. Despite the common misconception, marketing is more than advertising and promotion. In the past, companies were product-focused, employing teams of salespeople to push their products into or onto the market, regardless of market desire. A market-focused, or customer-focused, organization instead first determines what its potential customers desire, and then builds the product. The essence of marketing is the realization that customers use a product or service because they have a need, or because a product has perceived value, not because they want to spend their hard earned money. Using a vague definition of marketing fails to provide any direction to some one hoping to market his products or services effectively. With that, a more modern explanation of what marketing is—and what makes it effective—is a definition coined by marketing researcher and author Brian Norris. Two major aspects of marketing are the recruitment of new customers (acquisition) and the retention and expansion of relationships with existing customers (base management). Acquisition marketing is a four-step process that begins with analyzing and defining a qualified universe of potential users or buyers. After this phase in the marketing process, a true marketing effort succeeds in capturing the attention of the intended buyers within the targeted universe. Third, systematic effort must be put into getting the prospects to accept the concepts or propositions being offered via the marketing effort. Finally, with all three of the previous steps achieved, the marketer must convert prospective buyers into an actual buyers by getting them to take the desired action (purchase rent, call, download, subscribe, refer, sell, follow the law, become a member, etc.).

One a customer has converted the prospective buyer, base management marketing takes over. The process for base management shifts the marketer to building a relationship, nuturing the links, enhancing the benefits that sold the buyer in the first place and improving the products/service continuously to protect her business from competitive encroachments. Marketing methods are informed by many of the social sciences, particularly psychology, sociology, and economics. Marketing research underpins these activities. Through advertising, it is also related to many of the creative arts.

The word market originally meant the place where the exchange between seller and buyer took place. Todav we speak of a market as either a region where goods are sold and bought or particular types of buyer. When strategizing specialists in marketing comment about markets they are usually referring to the different groups of people and/or organizations. The four major market groups are (1) consumer, (2) business to business, (3) institutional, and (4) reseller.

The consumer market deals with the last/final customer who buys the product for their own satisfaction/personal use or household use. For example, If you were a college student consumer you could possibly be a member of the markets for "brand-name" clothing and shoes, college books, backpacks, newspapers and bicycles. You might also go to cafes, movie theatres and sports fixtures. The consumer market covers a wide variety of people of different ages, gender, race, etc. as long as they are also the end user of the product. The majority of advertising funds are spent on consumer markets.

In popular usage, the term "marketing" refers to the promotion of products, especially advertising and branding. However, in professional usage the term has a wider meaning that recognizes that marketing is customer centred. Products are often developed to meet the desires of groups of customers or even, in some cases, for specific customers. McCarthy divided marketing into four general sets of activities. His typology has become so universally recognized that, his four activity sets, the Four Ps, have passed into the language. The Four Ps are:

- Product: The Product management aspect of marketing deals with the specifications of the actual good or service, and how it relates to the enduser s needs and wants.
- Pricing: This refers to the process of setting a price for a product, including discounts.
- Promotion: This includes advertising, sales promotion, publicity, and personal selling, and refers to the various methods of promoting the product, brand, or company.
- Placement: Placement or distribution refers to how the product gets to the customer; for example, point of sale placement or retailing.

These four elements are often referred to as the marketing mix. A marketer can use these variables to craft a marketing plan. The four Ps model is most useful when marketing low value consumer products. Industrial products, services, high value consumer products require adjustments to this model. Services marketing must account for the unique nature of services. Industrial or b2b marketing must account for the long-term contractual agreements that are typical in supply chain transactions. Relationship marketing attempts to do this by looking at marketing from a long-term relationship perspective rather than individual transactions.

For a marketing plan to be successful, the mix of the four "P's" must reflect the wants and desires of the consumers in the target market. Trying to convince a market segment to buy something they do not want is extremely expensive and seldom successful. Marketers depend on marketing research, both formal and informal, to determine what consumers want and what they are willing to pay for. Marketers hope that this process will give them a sustainable competitive advantage. Marketing management is the practical application of this process. Most companies today have a customer orientation (also called customer focus). This implies that the company focuses its activities and products on customer needs. Generally there are two ways of doing this: the customer-driven approach and the product innovation approach. In the consumer-driven approach, consumer wants are the drivers of all strategic marketing decisions. No strategy is pursued until it passes the test of consumer research. Every aspect of a market ofering, including the nature of the product itself, is driven by the needs of potential consumers- The starting point is always the consumer. The rationale tor this approach is that there is no point spending R&D funds developing products that people will not buy. History attests to many products that were commercial failures inspite of being technological breakthroughs, in a product innovation approach, the company pursues product innovation, then tries to develop a market for the product. Product innovation drives the process and marketing research is conducted primarily to ensure that a profitable market segment(s) exists for the innovation. The rationale is that customers may not know what options will be available to them in the future so we should not expect them to tell us what they will buy in the future. It is claimed that if Thomas Edison depended on marketing research he would have produced larger candles rather than inventing light bulbs. Many firms, such as research and development focused companies, successfully focus on product innovation. Many purists doubt whether this is really a form of marketing orientation at all, because of the ex-post status of consumer research. Some even question whether it is marketing. Diffusion of innovations research explores how and why people adopt new products, services and ideas. A relatively new form of marketing uses the Internet and is called internet marketing or more generally e-marketing, affiliate marketing or online marketing. It typically tries to perfect the segmentation strategy used in traditional marketing. It targets its audience more precisely, and is sometimes called personalized marketing or one-to-one marketing.

COMPANY: AN INTRODUCTION

A company in the broadest sense is an aggregation of people who stay together for a common purpose. Such usage includes people assembled:

- For commercial or judicial purposes, organised as a type of business organization. See company (law) or the term corporation which may have the same meaning, depending on the jurisdiction.

CUSTOMER: AN INTRODUCTION

A customer is someone who purchases or rents something from an individual or organization. The word historically derives from "custom," meaning "habit"; a customer was someone who frequented a particular shop, who made it a habit to purchase goods of the sort the shop sold there rather than elsewhere, and with whom the shopkeeper had to maintain a relationship to keep his or her "custom," meaning expected purchases in the future. The shopkeeper remembered the sizes and preferences of his or her customers, for example. The word did not refer to those who purchased things at a fair or bazaar, or from a street vendor.

Customers can be classified into two main groups; internal and external customers. An internal customer is someone who works for the organisation, possibly in another department or another branch. External customers are essentially the general public. These two groups can be further broken down:

1. Internal Customers:
   - People working in different departments
   - People working in different branches
2. External Customers:
   - Individuals
   - Individuals of different needs
   - Individuals of different cultures
   - Business people
   - Groups

The customer thinks that because they are spending money with you it gives them the right to be rude. Church groups are the very worst.

Customers have needs and expectations that need to be observed by the organisation. A need is something that the customer needs, like car insurance being low. An expectation is something that the customer won't necessarily get but they expect to get, like a car getting from a person's place of departure to their destination. When they spend money with you once then they expect to get everything free after that.

Customer Care and Customer Relationship: Strategic Management and Support

A STRATEGIC FRAMEWORK FOR CUSTOMER RELATIONSHIP MANAGEMENT

Customer Relationship Management (CRM) is increasingly found at the top of corporate agendas. CRM is a management approach that seeks to create, develop and enhance relationships with carefully targeted customers in order to maximise customer value, corporate profitability and thus shareholder value, CRM is primarily concerned with utilising information technology to implement relationship marketing strategies. The emergence of CRM is a consequence of a number of trends:

- The shift in business focus from transactional marketing to relationship marketing
- The transition in structuring organisations, on a strategic basis, from functions to processes
- The recognition of the benefits of using information proactively rather than solely reactively
- The greater utilisation of technology in managing and maximising the value of information
- The realisation that customers are a business asset and not simply a commercial audience
- The acceptance of the need for trade-off between delivering and extracting customer value

While CRM represents a significant growth sector—current estimates place the world market for CRM at $US 5 billion—there is still considerable confusion surrounding the definition and role of CRM. This may be explained by:

- Its relatively recent and quick arrival as a management discipline
- The lack of a widely accepted and clear definition of its role and operation within the organisation

- An emphasis on information technology aspects rather than its benefits in terms of building relationships with customers
- The variety of CRM tools and services being offered by information technology vendors

To resolve this confusion and progress CRM, two major outstanding issues must be addressed: the need to approach CRM in a strategic, systematic manner and the need to fully understand what constitutes customer value. A Strategic Framework for CRM has been developed to help clarify CRM's function and 'fit' within the organisation, and to help optimise its use as a strategic management approach. This framework is comprised of five interrelated cross-functional processes:

- Strategic development process
- Value creation process
- Multi-channel integration process
- Information management process
- Performance assessment process

While these processes have universal application, the extent to which they are formalised by applying the framework will need to vary according to each organisation's unique situation.

This illustration sets out to provide a strategic framework tor understanding and implementing Customer Relationship Management (CRM) as an effective means of ensuring the overall business strategy delivers increased shareholder results. CRM is a relatively new discipline aimed at increasing the acquisition and retention of profitable customers by uniting the potential of IT and relationship marketing strategies. Companies large and small across a variety of sectors are increasingly embracing CRM as a major element of corporate strategy for two important reasons: (1) new technologies now enable companies to large! chosen market segments, micro-segments or individual customers more precisely; and (2) new marketing thinking has recognised the limitations of tradtional marketing and the potential of more customer-focused process-oriented perspectives. The urgent need to find alternative routes to competitive advantage has been driven by profound changes in the business environment, including: the growth and diversity of competition; the development and availability of new technology; the escalating expectations and empowerment of the individual; the advent of a global operating environment; and the erosion of conventional timeframes in this electronic-enabled era, That CRM offers a realistic and relevant response to these mounting challenges is evidenced by market demand Research by The Meta Group indicates that investment in CRM will grow from $US 5 billion in 2000 to $US 20 billion in 2004. However, CRM's recognised potential to deliver commercial improvement is currently curtailed by a lack of clear guidance on wha t CRM is and how it can be applied successfully. CRM's emphasis on the utilisation of IT, which in itself is a fast-evolving phenomenon, and on adopting a long-term, proactive perspective to customer management has resulted in considerable confusion about the exact definition and role of CRM within the organisation. To some it means direct mail or a loyalty card scheme, to others a help desk or a call centre. Still others see it as *a* relational database for key account management. As a result, many organisations are adopting CRM on a fragmented basis. The specific purpose of this article is to position CRM as a strategic set of activities that commences with a detailed review of an organisation's strategy and concludes with an improvement in shareholder value. The notion that competitive advantage stems from the creation of value for the customer and for the company is key to the success of CRM, which demands that responsibility for value delivery is shared across functions and hierarchies. Because CRM is a cross-functional activity and in large companies seeks to focus on potentially millions of individual customer relationships simultaneously, it can be unwieldy to implement and impossible to get right without a purposeful and systematic approach.

The Strategic Framework for CRM presented in Figure A is based on the interaction of five crossfunctional business processes that deal with strategy development, value creation, multi-channel integration, information management, and performance assessment.

These processes make a greater contribution to organisational prosperity collectively than they can individually, and must therefore be treated as an integrated and iterative set of activities Repeated consideration of each of the processes, moving essentially from left to right, will serve to continually develop the benefits oi CRM. To understand what these benefits are and how they are manifested, it is necessary to consider each of the processes, and the key questions they address, in turn.

The strategic framework for CR

1. Strategy Development Process

Most companies today recognise that their future depends on the strength of their business relationships, and most crucially, their relationships with customers. In an effort to effect better customer relationship management, many organisations are quickly introducing particular technologies in order to break the bonds of antiquated legacy systems and outmoded organisational cultures— often with disappointing outcomes. CRM, however, is not simply an IT solution to the problem of getting the right customer base and growing it. CRM is much more. Rather than turning immediately to technology, managers need to consider CRM in the context of overall business strategy. CRM will be one of perhaps many management approaches operating within the organisation and, like any other discipline, it must actively reflect and reinforce the wider goals of the business if it is to be successful. The strategy development process therefore demands a dual focus on the organisation's business strategy and its customer strategy: how well the two interrelate will fundamentally affect the success of the CRM strategy.

Business Strategy

A comprehensive review of the business strategy will provide a realistic platform on which to construct the CRM strategy, as well as generate recommendations for general improvement. The organisation needs to fully understand its own competencies within a competitive context in order to be able to transfer them to the customer as customer value. It is also vital that everyone in the organisation is pulling in the same, strategic direction, and that they are alert to changes which might signal opportunity or disaster. This is especially important where the organisation is in transition from a product orientation to customer orientation. Consideration of the following key business issues, present and future, will serve to re-affirm the appropriate course and direction for the organisation:

- Company's profile, purpose, performance and position
- Stage of the industry's evolution
- Competitor profiles and activity
- Delivery channels
- Information technology platform

Customer Strategy

The other half of the strategy equation is deciding which customers the business wants most to attract and to keep, and which customers it would prefer to be without. No firm can successfully be 'all things to all people', and thus finding your best potential customers and retaining them is vital. While the prior review of business strategy will be instrumental in reaching a judgement on broad customer focus, consideration of following customer issues will help to refine customer selection and thus customer strategy.

- Nature and status of customer strategy
- Customer segments
- Customer relationships
- Knowledge of and value of customer base
- Product/service involvement and complexity of purchasing behaviour

Creating competitive advantage through the skilful management of customer relationships will normally require a reappraisal of the way in which customers are approached and segmented, and the way in which resources are allocated and used. Determining the appropriate degree of customer segmentation, or segment granularity, be it at a macro, micro or one-to-one level, is clearly a prerequisite for progressing to the value creation process.

2. Value Creation Process

The value creation process is concerned with transforming the outputs of the strategy development process into programmes that both extract and deliver value. An insufficient focus on the value provided to key customers, as opposed to the money obtained from them, can seriously dimmish the impact of the offer in terms of its perceived value. A balanced value exchange will ensure that both parties enjoy a good return on investment, leading to a good relationship.

The value creation process consists of three key elements: determining what value the company can provide to its customers (the 'value customer receives'); determining the value of the organisation receives from its customers (the 'value organisation receives'); and, by successfully managing this value exchange, maximising the lifetime value of desirable customer segments.

The Value the Customer Receives

The value the customer receives from the supplier organisation is the total package of benefits derived from the 'core product' and the 'product surround', or the added values that enhance the basic features such as service and support. The value the customer attributes to these benefits is in proportion to the perceived ability of the offer to solve whatever customer problem prompted the purchase. This value can be calculated using the value proposition concept and undertaking a value assessment— importantly, working from a customer perspective.

The Value Proposition

The aim of all businesses is to create a value proposition for customers, be it implicit or explicit, which is superior to and more profitable than those of competitors. In specific usage, a 'value proposition' is the offer defined in terms of the target customers, the benefits offered to these customers, and the price charged relative to the competition. Value propositions explain the relationship between the performance of the product, the fulfilment of the customer's needs and the total cost to the customer over the customer relationship life cycle. As every customer is different and has changing needs, it is crucial that the value proposition for each customer is clearly and individually articulated, and cognisant of the customer's lifetime value.

The Value Assessment

To determine if the value proposition is likely to result in a superior customer experience, it is necessary to quantify the relative importance that customers place upon the various attributes of a product. A value assessment based on subjective judgements about the attributes and benefits that are important to the customer can fall prey to the assumption that the supplier and customer attach the same importance to the various product attributes—rarely do they. A more realistic evaluation can be obtained by asking a representative sample of customers to rank the product's attributes. Then, using an analytical tool such as conjoint analysis, or tradeoff analysis, a weighting system can be applied to discover the weight given to different levels of each attribute. Conjoint analysis can also be used to identify customers that share common preferences in terms of product attributes, and may reveal substantial market segments with service needs that are not fully catered for by existing offers.

The Value the Organisation Receives

The value the company receives from the customer is an output of, rather than an input to, value creation. As such, it focuses not on the creation of value for the customer but on the value outcome that can be derived from delivering superior customer value. The pursuit of more, and more attractive, customers at lower cost must be based on a sound understanding of how acquisition costs vary at both the segment and channel levels. In many instances customer acquisition can be improved through insights drawn from the value proposition and the value assessment. More refined promotional campaigns and the encouragement of customer referrals can also attract new customers who meet the target criteria. The activity of keeping and growing existing custom is fast becoming a business priority. Since the publication of Reicheld's and Sasser's dramatic findings which clearly linked retention to profitability, many authors and researchers have suggested that it costs around five times more to get a new customer than it does to keep an existing one. While the financial implications of emphasising customer retention to an extent greater than, or least equal to, customer acquisition are significant, remarkably few companies have reacted to benefit from this knowledge. One explanation may be found in an ingrained organisational culture that rewards customer acquisition much more than customer retention.

Customer Segment Lifetime Value Analysis

To decide the relative amount of emphasis that should be placed on customer acquisition and customer retention, it is necessary to understand acquisition and retention economics at segment, or better yet, individual, level. The key metric used to evaluate customers' profit potential is customer lifetime value (CLV), which is defined as the net present value of the future profit flow over a customer's lifetime, or the duration of the account. Some analysts have developed models, such as The Retentiongram Model, to help identify CLV for customer segments in specific businesses. Having mastered CLV modelling, organisations can then advance to modelling future profit potential, which may be used to identify means of enhancing profitability through a variety of approaches including the creative use of alternative channels.

3. The Multi-Channel Integration Process

The multi-channel integration process involves decisions about the most appropriate combination of channels; how to ensure the customer experiences highly positive interactions within those channels; and, where the customer interacts with more than one channel, how to create and present a 'single unified view' of the customer. To determine the nature of the business's customer interface, it is necessary to consider the key issues underlying channel selection; the purpose of multi-channel integration; the channel options available; and the importance of integrated channel management in delivering an outstanding customer experience.

Issues in Channel Selection

Channel suitability: The most appropriate choice of channel (or channels) for any company will be the one that is most attractive, in terms of value, to the end consumers in the target market segment. The level of attractiveness will be determined by the company's ability to create customer value relevant to those customers' needs. By identifying which benefits the customer seeks and the relative importance attributed to them, the company can evaluate channel suitability and determine which channel option would deliver these benefits to the greatest degree and for the lowest cost. Channel structure: The way in which the channel is organised can seriously influence the success or failure of the channel. Over the last decade, the traditional channel structures of many industries have been dismantled and reconfigured in response to new technologies that have opened alternative or improved paths to market. Disintermediation and reintermediation are two important types of structural change that need to be considered in detail.

Multi-channel Integration

Faced with the necessity of offering consumers different channel types to meet their changing needs during the sales cycle (pre sale, sale, and post sale), it is increasingly imperative to integrate the activities in those different channels to produce the most positive customer experience and to create the maximum value, no matter what channel is being used. Discussions on channels are usually dominated by those who are involved in making the sale. However, for strategic CRM the channels need to be seen in the context of the whole interaction over the life cycle of the customer relationship, not just in terms of the specific sales activity.

Channel Options

Within these typical stages, a great number of interactions occur between the customer and the organisation across different channels. The multi-channel integration process should therefore start with the identification of the most appropriate channel options for specific segments. These options fall into six main channel categories, ranging from the physical to the virtual.

Although there are many individual channel options, it is convenient to group them into these six categories. Thus options such as retail branches and kiosks are included within 'outlets' and telephone contact; call centres and fax within 'telephony'; and the internet and digital TV within 'e-commerce'. E-commerce and m-commerce are addressed separately, as the ubiquity of the mobile device, future technology advances beyond the existing WAP (wireless application protocol) technology and the ability to tailor information based on the customer's physical location justify the latter being considered in its own right. Some channels will be employed in combination to maximise commercial exposure and return, for example, 'voice over IP' (voice over internet protocol) integrates both telephony and the internet.

Integrated Channel Management

Managing integrated channels relies on the ability to uphold the same high standards across multiple, different channels. Having established a set of standards for each channel used, which defines an outstanding customer experience for that channel, the organisation can then work to integrate the channels, trying to optimise but not comprise the accepted channel standards. The multi-channel service must match the individual (and changing) needs of customers, who may belong to a number of different customer segments simultaneously. To succeed, the company must be able to gather and deploy customer knowledge from the different channels as well as other sources.

4. Information Management Process

The information management process is concerned with the collection and collation of customer information from all customer contact points; and the utilisation of this information to construct complete and current customer profiles which can be used to enhance the quality of the customer experience. As companies grow and interact with an increasing number of customers through an increasing diversity of channels, the need for a systematic approach to organising and employing information becomes ever greater. In an effort to keep pace with escalating volumes of data, the tendency is for organisations to create more or bigger databases within functions or departments, leading to a fragmented and often unwieldy body of information upon which to make crucial management decisions. The elevation of CRM from a specific application such as a call centre, to a pan-company strategy requires the integration of all customer interactions. The key material elements of the information management process are the data repository and analytical tools; IT systems; and front office and back office applications.

Data Repository

The data repository provides a powerful corporate memory of customers, an integrated enterprise-wide data store capable of relevant data analyses. It consists of databases and a data warehouse, or a collection of related databases that are brought together so that the maximum value can be extracted from them. An enterprise data model is used to manage this data conversion process, in order to minimise data duplication and to resolve any inconsistencies between databases. As well as connecting to internal systems, the data warehouse often takes feeds from external sources.

Through the effective use of analytical tools, such as data mining and market segmentation analysis, the data warehouse can help in identifying the most promising customers, and finding ways to retain them and enhance their value. It can also support the monitoring of customers and provide a mechanism for testing and refining customer strategy. This capability is increasingly significant as markets become ever more dynamic, and personalised services and one-to-one marketing become more commonplace.

Analytical Tools

The analytical tools that enable effective use of the data warehouse can be found in general data mining packages and in specific software application packages. Data mining packages enable the analysis of large quantities of data to discover meaningful patterns and relationships. Each pattern and relationship explains something about customer behaviour and provides indications of how customer relationships can be improved. More specific software application packages include analytical tools that focus on such tasks as: campaign management analysis, credit scoring and customer profiling. These task-specific software packages combine several of the general functions of data mining with support for the task that will not be found in general data mining software.

IT Systems

IT systems refer to the computer hardware and the related software and middleware used within the organisation. Often some technology integration is required before databases can be integrated into a data warehouse and user access can be provided across the company. IT systems must be able to deliver the information needed on customers both now and in the future, and to accomplish other administrative duties. The organisation's capacity to scale existing systems or plan for the migration to larger systems without disrupting business operations is critical. So too is the integration of data from highly contrasting systems, such as structured databases and rich multi-media networks.

Front Office and Back Office Applications

Front-office applications are the technologies used to support all those activities that involve direct interface with customers, including sales force automation (SFA) and call-centre management. These applications are used to increase revenues by improving customer retention and raising sales closure rates. Back-office applications support internal administration activities and supplier relationships, involving human resources, procurement, warehouse management, logistics software and some financial processes. Some marketing activities, such as campaign management, are difficult to classify because they are customer-facing, but do not directly support interactions with the customer. The growth of enterprise-wide systems and e-business is also blurring the distinction between front-office and back-office, and challenging the structure and operation of existing information management processes. A key concern about front- and back-office systems is that they are sufficiently connected and co-ordinated to optimise customer relations and workflow. Clearly, the information management process is playing an increasingly important role in CRM, supporting the collection, analysis and use of enormous volumes of complex customer data. Since customer data has a limited shelf life, it is crucial that it is accumulated and deployed in an organised and integrated manner to provide a current and comprehensive view of customers, Selecting the appropriate IT hardware, software and systems to achieve this can be a challenging task, given the constraints of legacy systems, the enormous range of technology options, and the uniqueness of every business situation. The growing variety of CRM tools and services on offer from IT vendors further complicates the questions of what constitutes the best CRM solution and whether to source the IT infrastructure externally or to construct it using internal expertise. Whatever option, or combination of options, is pursued, the underlying principle is that the IT infrastructure should create a 'nerve centre', integrating disparate customer data into customer interactions. To ensure that technology solutions support CRM, it is important to conduct IT planning from a perspective of providing a seamless customer service, rather than planning for functional or product-centred departments and activities. Such a customer-centred approach to IT planning will ensure that customer information is used effectively to maximise customer value and the profitability of each customer. Furthermore, data analysis tools, such as those outlined above, make it possible to measure business activities to determine whether new ways of managing customer relationships might be advantageous in increasing shareholder value. This kind of analysis provides the basis for the performance assessment process.

5. The Performance Assessment Process

The performance assessment process ensures that the organisation's strategic aims in terms of CRM are being delivered to an appropriate and acceptable standard, and that a basis for future improvement is established. Figure A shows the two main elements of this: shareholder results which provides a 'macro' view of the overall relationships that drive performance; and performance monitoring which gives a more detailed 'micro' view of metrics and key performance indicators.

Performance Assessment

Shareholder Results

To achieve the ultimate objective of CRM—the delivery of shareholder results through an increase in shareholder value— the organisation must possess an in-depth understanding of the four key drivers of shareholder results within the context of the business strategy and the customer strategy set out earlier. They are: building employee value; building customer value; building shareholder value; and reducing costs.

Employee Value, Customer Value and Shareholder Value

Recent examination of the relationship between employees, customers and shareholders has highlighted the need to adopt a more informed and integrated approach to exploiting the linkages between them. The 'linkage model' in Figure B illustrates the connection between good leadership and management behaviour, improved employee attitudes, consistent customer satisfaction,, and increased sales, profits and shareholder results.

The Linkage Model

Most managers, however, have no idea how much an improvement in one variable will lead to a measurable increase in another. To resolve this problem, specific linkage models such as the 'service profit chain model' developed by researchers at the Harvard Business School are being devised. As a result, more companies are now starting to recognise the value of addressing these higher-level drivers before determining standards, metrics and key performance indicators.

Cost Reduction

The two means of cost reduction most relevant to CRM are: deploying electronic systems, such as automated telephony services, which lower costs by enabling reductions in staff and overheads; and utilising new electronic channels, such as online self-service facilities, which lower the costs of customer acquisition, transaction and servicing. However, an over concentration on cost reduction as a means of delivering shareholder results can be counterproductive if it decreases customer value. For example, the creation of a central call centre in a bank will reduce costs but may disenfranchise customers who prefer to interact with bank employees whom they know Thus any cost reduction strategy needs to be considered in the context of its effect on customer value.

Performance Monitoring

Despite the increasing focus on customer-facing activities, there is growing concern that metrics generally used by companies for CRM are not nearly as advanced as they should be. In particular, more detailed standards, measures and key performance indicators are needed to ensure CRM activities are planned and practised effectively, and that a feedback loop exists to maximise performance improvement and organisational learning.

Standards

The current lack of an internationally recognised set of standards for CRM has hindered efforts to measure and benchmark CRM performance. However, a number of initiatives are under way, such as the COPC Standard for call centres and the BT initiative to identify best practice standards for key areas across the CRM Strategic Framework.

Metrics, KPIs and Results

Traditional performance measurement and monitoring systems, which tend to be functionally driven, are inappropriate for the cross-functional and holistic management approach of CRM. Metrics and key performance indicators (KPIs) for CRM must adequately reflect the performance standards across the five major CRM processes, and also, the linkages between these metrics and KPI's must be leveraged to secure improved results through improved CRM management.

Recent efforts to provide cross-functional measures, such as the 'balanced scorecard' approach, are a useful step forward but are not yet well-enough developed to address the complexities of CRM. Until further research is undertaken we suggest organisations should focus on four key categories of measurement for CRM: strategic metrics, customer metrics, operational metrics and output metrics.

The strategic framework for CRM presented in this article is a formal response to the confusion and frustration many companies are experiencing in their efforts to adopt CRM. By breaking CRM down into several manageable processes, it is possible to communicate the underlying principles of CRM and to demonstrate the interdependence of CRM activities. This framework should be approached with an open mind, applied with an element of flexibility and modified where appropriate, as no two organisations will share the same circumstances. It is also meant to be applied iteratively, with organisational learning being applied to continually refine the CRM strategy in the light of experiences in using the framework. It is also worth emphasising that the successful implementation of CRM requires visible top-level backing and the full commitment of the workforce and other partners throughout the supply chain. No amount of IT can compensate for the requirement of human investment. This is evident in the goal of CRM: to create a seamless personalised customer experience that is consistently and continually enhanced. For desirable customers, anything less is inappropriate. Those companies that offer strong personalisation and consistently high standards of service based on all of the customer's interactions, regardless of channel, will have considerable advantage over those that operate from disparate silos of customer information. CRM demands coordination and collaboration, and most of all integration: integration of information and information systems to provide business intelligence; integration of channels to enable the development and delivery of a single unified view of the customer; integration of resources, functions and processes to ensure a productive, customer-oriented working environment and competitive organisational performance. CRM is admittedly a complex task, but with a strategic approach, as outlined here, organisations should be able to better realise the huge benefits of effective CRM.

CUSTOMER CARE AND RELATIONSHIP SUPPORT OFFICE (CARUSO)

Customer Relationship Management (CRM) is an inherent business strategy for companies big and small. The technology has reached a point where it is truly enabling the way enterprises manage their customer relationships. The goal of the EU funded project CARUSO is the design of a software toolkit that facilitates the building and maintaining of high quality business-to-business and business-to-customer relationships. CARUSO is designed to allow a multi-imensional way of looking at markets, customers, suppliers, products, personnel, internal and external information, communication and action flow. This will be accomplished by the following core features: front-office application builder with customer care and marketing desk, basic technologies comprising a general communication server, intelligent information, document and contact access, unified messaging, and a customizable user interface. Emphasis will be put on exploiting existing tool packages as much as possible. The CARUSO toolkit is targeted at European Small and Medium Sized Enterprises (SME) and allows them to optimize their business operations to the mutual benefit of both the supplier and the consumer.

Introduction

Currently European SMEs are affected by major changes in global economics. In the US millions of jobs were lost in the 1980s which led to the metamorphosis from a product(ion) oriented to a service oriented market by which millions of new service jobs were created. A similar development is now going on in Europe.

It has been realized that gaining new customers is much .more expensive than keeping the current customers. Companies are fighting for the same customers, but, at the same time, customers are finding that it is very easy to switch from one company to another. The financial impact of customers disloyalty can be immense. A recent Harvard University study reported that in many companies a five per cent improvement in customer retention could increase profits by 85 per cent. Therefore, it is no wonder that companies are searching for ways to reduce customer turnover. Recent surveys have also shown that poor service or inattention is the cause of 65 per cent of customers leaves.

Thus, keeping customers or increasing their loyalty can be achieved by focusing on their needs. As a result, companies are trying to improve the quality of customer interaction and the service of customer requests, starting with the very first contact, and on throughout the sales process to the service and support provided after the initial sale or service.

Customer Relationship Management (CRM) is an inherent business strategy used to achieve this goal. This relatively new concept influences strategy, business processes, as well as information systems in many companies. CRM and a high quality supplier relationship are essential success factors in a highly competitive global marketplace.

In the past, business relationship management was both cost and time intensive. In particular SMEs, with naturally limited resources, were not in a position to carry out broad-scale marketing programmes or administer their supplier relationships in a effective way. Now, technology has reached a point where it is truly enabling the way enterprises manage their business relationships.

The market trend is to cover the definition of CRM with a single integrated platform. Island solutions like customer care, support, and contact management cannot fulfill the CRM demands. For example, Siebel (Siebel 2000) bought Scopus Technologies to integrate customer service technology in their products. Other companies have signed co-operation agreements or developed modules, interfaces, respectively in joint efforts. Having their origin in backoffice applications such as accounting, purchasing, and production, Oracle (Oracle 2000), BAAN (Baan 2000), or SAP (SAP 2000) follow with their strategy this path to integrate the missing building blocks for customer relationship.

The EU-project CARUSO (Customer Care and Relationship Support Office) aims at providing European SMEs with a tool package that provides the flexibility of individually built applications tailored to their specific needs in the field of customer and supplier relationship management. It is also going to facilitate business strategies which will help to understand and anticipate the needs of an enterprise's current and potential customers. Another objective of CARUSO is to provide the technology that helps to grow customers into a position of equivalent partners who will pro-actively influence the life-cycle of goods and services including areas such as pre sales, marketing, post sales, and maintenance. Thus customers will gain a more direct influence on the nature and quality of products and services offered including the provision of all relevant information to them.

The CRM Challenge

The ultimate goal of CRM is to attract and retain customers and increase the profits. CRM is a complex process that requires, on one hand, a redesign of current business processes and, on the other hand, integrated IT support. The key factor is how well an organization manages its customer relationships from the first contact through the sales process, customer service, and ongoing customer retention activities.

In recent years, call centres have gained popularity as being cost-effective and efficient. Organizations are now realizing the critical importance of every customer contact and the potential of the call centre for customer relationship management strategies. The proper application of call centres can improve the overall quality of customer interaction while streamlining customer requests and orders. In addition, call centres are nowadays increasingly responsible for business interactions that are being conducted through alternative emerging communications channels, such as e-mail, internet, fax, voice mail, pager, etc.

One of the most urgent challenge facing call centres today is the fact that it is becoming increasingly difficult and costly to recruit, train, and retain qualified call centre agents. Technology is a key to help reduce the learning time and costs of call centre employees. Moreover, technology can help inexperienced representatives deliver much better customer service.

Another important issue is equipping agents with the necessary empowerment and competence to allow him or her making proper decisions without unnecessary call escalation. Call escalations are usually very time and resource consuming and decrease the customer satisfaction; therefore it is desirable to avoid them as much as possible. One way to achieve this is implementing some form of unified agent desktop application to give call centre agents the information they need to respond quickly and accurately to customer questions and requests. Another, more important way, is to integrate the agent desktop system with knowledge-bases and back office systems as well as with the company's business strategies. This will help save time, for example, by automatically retrieving customer account information from the corporate database and displaying it on an agent's desktop.

A growing number of call centres are also considering the use of sales configuration to help automate the sales process. These are often provided by rule-based engines which help to translate customer needs into sales opportunities and, at the same time, simplify the selling of complex products and services. By the means of sales configuration technology, companies can rapidly roll out new campaigns. This technology also allows inexperienced agents and even new hires to present very complex products and services and to interact with the company workflows.

All the technical means cannot and should not eliminate the personal relationship with the customers. The ability for call centre agents to view the information about the customer can help maintain a more personal interaction. Current script generators enable call centre agents to create personalized, one-to-one correspondence based upon the customer's profile and information gathered during the contact so that the company presents one face to the customer.

Another emerging challenge is the fact that call centres must be able to address multiple contact channels including phone, fax, postal services, internet, e-mail, voice mail, etc. In fact, many call centres are developing into multimedia communication centres. Companies are integrating their call centres with their web pages to enable customers to help themselves as well as to schedule callbacks or initiate on-line chat sessions with customer service representatives. This allows customers to use the way they prefer to contact and interact with companies. Therefore, organizations are looking for unified messaging solutions to help manage the flow of interactions across the various communication channels.

One of the key aspects of CRM is that it is centred around the customer and not around the departments of the company. Usually this implies that the business processes that are needed for dealing with a customer cross the boundary of single departments or business units. It is crucial that business workflows in a call centre can be integrated with the back office workflows, and that the workflows can be modified appropriately if needed. Workflow automation software allows for directing and monitoring work that goes outside of the call centre to assure completion or tracking progress. This helps reduces fulfillment time of new product orders and allows call centre agents to be better informed of the current status of a customer request.

To effectively deal with customers, a CRM system needs to store customer profile information in addition to a complete customer contact history, including any documentation that is associated with the customer. This can increase revenues through improved cross-selling and up-selling capabilities, and, moreover, they help companies improve their understanding of buying patterns and customer preferences as well as the targeting of their marketing efforts.

However, maintaining this information can pose considerable problems because usually this information is spread throughout the different IT systems of an organization, and it exists in a range of formats. Further, to be effective, it is important that only the information necessary to deal with the customer's current issue is retrieved, while unnecessary information is suppressed.

The American market research company AMR Research estimates the total size of the world-wide CRM market at more than $2.5 billion in 1998, and growing at more than 50 per cent a year. This does not include software from vendors who incorporate CRM functions in their core products. The major players in the CRM market segment are Siebel, Vantive, Clarify, Point, Applix (APPLIX 2000), Corepoint, and IMA (cf. (MSI 2000)). Remedy offers a solution for call centres with very powerful workflow engine (Remedy 1999). Newcomers from the USA originating from internet based applications, like Pivotal, Firebond, Upshot, and Vignette, try to break into the CRM market segment now. The market leader in CRM, following AMR, is Siebel Systems founded only a few years ago. Siebel is the largest player in the market, a position they have achieved by focusing on large accounts and not on SMEs. Siebel's deals are typically in the millions of dollars. Its closest competitor is Vantive; the two have about 25 per cent of the market.

The CRM market in Europe is still immature. Outside of large corporations little has been done, and even there the market is scarcely beyond its infancy. New companies have started to move in which indicates that the market has reached the critical growth phase. These companies include SalesLogix, Onyx, Pivotal, Firebond, Upshot, and Vignette. Their

CRM systems mostly evolved from existing contact management systems and internet based applications for small- to medium-sized businesses. One problem with these systems is that they address the needs of the US market rather than the needs of European companies,

A lot of the currently offered software packages fulfill only part of the CRM demands. SFA (Sales Force Automation) is the predecessor of CRM. They focus on sales and marketing application, primarily for the sales force (help desk, complaint management, telemarketing) are gradually also offered by these packages. There are several players at the moment like Siebel, Remedy, Scopus, Heat, Clarify, Vantive, Point, Cincom, and many others.

Usually the costs for adapting CRM software to the business processes of a company is much bigger than the costs of the software itself. This is the reason why currently the major players address the Fortune 500 enterprises only. The software packages represent a major investment. For example, a Clarify solution is a million project and only suited for a minimum of 50-100 agents. On the other hand, in particular newly funded small companies require highly integrated and powerful instruments to establish a solid customer base.

Project Objectives

Building and ensuring high quality of supplier consumer relationships is the prime objective of this project by means of a Customer Care and Relationship Support Office (CARUSO). CARUSO provides management and control tools to monitor and improve European SMEs relationship to customers.

The goal of CARUSO is the generation of a software tool-kit that facilitates the building of highly scalable front-office applications to maintain high quality consumer-supplier relationships. Emphasis will be put on exploiting and integrating existing tool packages as much as possible.

The installation of many CRM systems is very expensive because specialists are needed to adapt the core system to the needs of the company. This makes the use of CRM less suitable for SMEs, CARUSO addresses this problem by providing an easy to use application builder, which allows the rapid generation of front-office applications tailored to the individual requirements of a company. A script developer is integrated into the application builder to provide conversation scripts to aid and guide the agent. The script developer offers immediate modification options to respond to, for instance, specific campaign requirements.

Since many of the relevant data dealing with customers are spread among the IT systems of a company, CARUSO provides interfaces to the company's Enterprise Resource Planning (ERP) systems and other installed software applications, and provides interface options for the most common used data bases. In particular interfaces to back-office systems allows the design of front-office applications that provide a unified access to the back-office functionality. This is achieved by representing databases, ERP systems, and back office applications as software components using standard middleware technologies like CORBA, COM/ DCOM, or Enterprise Java Beans (EJB).

To protect the companies investment into their Private Branch Exchange (PBX) systems, CARUSO makes use of the installed basis of the PBX by providing a Computer Telephone Integration (CTI) module which is compatible to nearly all available European PBX systems, offering in addition the functionality of Interactive Voice Responder (IVR), and Voice-Mail-Server as well as Power-Dialer.

Another aspect targeted by CARUSO is the integration of different communication channels, like phone, e-mail, fax, web, etc. in a Unified Messaging System, which allows consistent communication with the customers in a variety of ways.

CARUSO provides adaptation of front-office functions based on customer profile and contact history by means of a dynamic graphical user interface (GUI), and skill-based call distribution taking into account the agent's tasks and expertise. This allows a more efficient interaction with the customer by providing the help desk agent with only the functionality needed to resolve the customer's issue. Further, the interaction will he guided using information about solutions to frequently occurring problems stored in a knowledge base.

In addition, the CARUSO toolkit has the following crucial features:
- Full support for workflow, document, and contact management
- Web interface for the help desk agent which allows rapid dissemination of adapted or new front-office applications, and a similar interface to the one used by the help desk agent can be used for the customer (self help)
- A solution that is geared to European standards and requirements rather than US', in particular multilingual support

- A management information and control system that allows to monitor customer satisfaction and the effectiveness of the CRM processes, and provides data mining functions to identify customer behaviour patterns.

The Architecture of CARUSO

The architecture of CARUSO consists of three layers: the front-office layer, the middleware layer, and the basic technologies layer. The front-office layer contains the front-office applications which are designed and customized by using the tools of the development toolbox. The development toolbox contains, among others, the application builder and the script developer.

The basic technology layer consists of a general communication server; office applications; information, document, and contact databases; and a unified messaging server. The communication server manages various communication media (e.g. telephone, text, data, fax, e-mail, www, video), and is prepared not only for voice over the internet protocol (IP), but also for IP call centre functionality. The task of the middleware layer is the integration of the communication services with the other basic technology components and the front-office applications. The middleware layer provides a uniform access to customer data and history stored in the various databases of an enterprise, like contact databases and ERP systems CORBA, EJB, and COM/DCOM are used for the middleware components and services.

The component based approach together with the development toolbox makes it possible to extend CARUSO with new interfaces to basic technologies and allows the generation of customer care applications tailored to the individual enterprise requirements. Further, it is possible to start with only a tew components and add new components as needed.

The overall design of CARUSO follows an iterative object-oriented approach based on the Unified Modeling Language (UML) (Booch et al. 1999) and the Unified Process (Jacobson et al. 1999). Within the last few years the UML has become the standard notation for object oriented modelling. The UML is a diagrammatic notation for modelling object-oriented software systems. Class, component, and deployment diagrams model the static aspect of software systems, while Use Case, interaction, and activity diagrams are used to model the dynamic aspects.

The UML can be used with any object-oriented software development method; it itself does not constitute a development method. For CARUSO we have chosen the Unified Process.

Within one release cycle, the Unified Process distinguishes four phases: inception, elaboration, construction, and transition. The goal of the inception phase is to establish the business case, the goal of the elaboration phase is a project plan and a sound architecture, the goal of the construction phase is the final system, and the goal of the transition phase is to deliver the system to its end users. Within each of the four phases the basic workflows business modelling, requirements, analysis and design, implementation, test, and deployment are executed, possibly several times.

The advantage of this approach is that at the end of each iteration the result is a running system which allows for immediate feedback. Immediate feedback is important because it is very hard, if possible at all, to gain a relatively precise and complete specification of a system as complex as a CRM system in one big step. Only by testing successive versions of the system, missing and inappropriate functionality can be discovered.

Conclusion

In this article we have given an overview of the EU funded project CARUSO. The project is pursued by a group of companies that cover the role of end user, technology provider, software developers, and methodology provider.

The role of the end user is played by REMU who wants to apply CARUSO to maintain relations with its customers, REMU is a Dutch energy provider that supplies electricity, gas, and heating.

Data Call Systeme GmbH is a software house with sites in Munich, Munster and Paris. The key competence of DataCall is the integration of different communication media into information systems in order to facilitate work processes at multimedia workstations.

SFI, a Portuguese software company, is specialized in high-performance application development, creating tailor-made software solutions.

The Institut fur Informatik of the University of Munich acts in the project as the methodology provider which develops the overall architecture and controls the technical design.

The CARUSO project started in the beginning of 2000 and is scheduled for a period of two years. In the moment of writing the project has completed the inception phase and is in the middle of the elaboration phase. We are currently working on a prototype showing the key features of CARUSO.

Among presentations and demonstrations on tradeshows, distributing press releases and publishing best practice reports, an user interest group will be used to exploit and disseminate the results of the project. The group will consist of industrial and institutional partners who will use and test CARUSO. After completion of the final tool, these partners will provide an adequate reference as a basis for the further dissemination of the results. The initial user interest group will consist of SMEs from Europe. It is planned to enlarge this group towards the final prototype phase to build the basis for an early and effective dissemination.

ROLE OF INFORMATION TECHNOLOGY

Information Technology (IT) or Information and Commumcation(s) Technology (ICT) is the technology required for information processing. In particular the use of electronic computers and computer software to convert, store, protect, process, transmit, and retrieve information from anywhere, anytime. "Communications" is often used in the sigular, i.e. without an s, in this context. Apparently many people feel that the plural is unnecessary and pedantic or even bad English, and the term without the S is about twice as common as with it on all Internet sites, all UK sites, all US university and other edu sites, and all UK sites that also have the word "university." However, most dictionaries make a distinction between communication and communications, and in any case, the person and the report who coined the term ICT and first used it also used it in the plural.

Major IT topics include:

- Information technology audit
- Computing
- Computer science
- Information science
- Information security
- Worldwide web
- Digital library
- Pattern recognition
- Data management
    - Data processing
    - RFID
    - Data mining
    - Data drilling
    - Metadata a

- Data storage
    - Database
    - Data networking
- Technology assessment
- Cryptography
- Information technology infrastructure library
- Information technology governance
- Telematics
- and many more...

ROLE OF CALL CENTRE

A call centre (Commonwealth English) or call rentre (AmE) is a centralized office of a company that answers incoming telephone calls from customers (often for the purposes of product support), or that makes outgoing telephone calls to customers (telemarketing). Such an office may also respond to letters, faxes, e-mails and similar written correspondence. However the term contact centre (Commonwealth English) or contact centre (AmE) is often applied when such multiple functions are blended in one office. Call centres are generally set up as large rooms, with work stations that include a computer, a telephone set (or headset) hooked into a large telecom switch and one or more supervisor stations. It may stand by itself or be linked with other centres. It may also be linked to a corporate computer network, including main frames, microcomputers and LANs. Increasingly, the voice and data pathways into the centre are linked through a set of new technologies called computer telephony integration (CTI). Most major businesses use call centres to interact with their customers. Examples include utility companies, mail order catalogue firms, and customer support for computer hardware and software. Some businesses even service internal functions though call centres. Examples include help desks and sales support.

Queueing theory mathematics can be used to demonstrate that a single large call centre is more effective at answering calls than several smaller centres. The most dramatic improvements come when a large number of offices are centralised. The mathematical problems encountered in a call centre are generally statistical in nature and revolve around the probability that an arriving call will be answered by an available and appropriately trained person. Forecasting the call arrival rates and then scheduling the number of staff required on duty at particular times of the day are challenging problems faced by most call centre managers,

The centralised approach aims to rationalise the company's operations and reduce costs, whilst producing a standard, branded, front to the world. The approach naturally lends itself to large companies with a large, distributed customer base. Owing to the size of companies and their customer bases, these offices are often very large, such as converted warehouses.

Centralised offices means that large numbers of workers can be managed and controlled by a relatively small number of managers and support staff. They are often supported by computer technology that manages, measures and monitors the performance and activities of the workers. Call centre staff are some of the most heavily monitored and tracked groups of workers in the world. Reporting and monitoring in a call centre can be broken down into four major categories. These are real time reporting, historical reporting, quality monitoring and work force management. The types of information collected for a group of call centre agents are inclusive of: agents logged in, agents ready to take calls, agents available to take calls, agents in wrap up mode, average call duration, average call duration including wrap-up time, longest duration agent available, longest duration call in queue, number of calls in queue, number of calls offered, number of calls abandoned, average speed to answer, average speed to abandoned and service level (the percentage of calls answered in under a certain time period). Many call centres use work force management software, which is software that uses historical information coupled with projected need to generate automated schedules that will provide the correct mixture of staff with the correct skills necessary to service customers.

Normally, personnel costs are the most significant expense of a call centre operation and even seemingly small inefficiencies can have significant cost issues. This is one of the major driving factors of outsourcing in the call centre industry. Inadequate computer systems can mean staff take one or two seconds longer than necessary to process a transaction. This can often be quantified in staff cost terms. This is often used as a driving factor in any business case to justify a complete system upgrade or replacement. For several factors, including the effeciency of the call centre, level of computer and telecom support that may be adequate for staff in a typical branch office may prove totally inadequate in a call centre.

Call Centres use a wide variety of different technologies to allow them to manage the large volumes of work that need to be managed by the call centre. These technogies ensure that agents are kept as productive as possible, and that calls are queued and processed as quickly as possible according to the desired levels of service.

These include:

- ACD (automatic call distribution)
- Agent performance analytics
- BTTC (best time to call)/Outbound call optimization
- IVR (interactive voice response)
- CTI (computer telephony integration)
- Enterprise campaign management
- Outbound predictive dialer
- CRM (customer relationship management)
- CIM (customer interaction management)
- E-mail management
- Chat and web collaboration
- Desktop scripting solutions
- TTS (text to speech)
- WFM (workforce management)
- Voice analysis
- Voice recognition
- Voicemail
- VoIP

Types of calls are often divided into outbound and inbound, Inbound calls are calls that are initiated by the customer to obtain information, report a malfunction or ask for help. This is substantially different from outbound calls where the agent initiates the call to a customer mostly with the aim to sell a product or a service to that customer. The staff of a call centre that is focused on support of a product is often organized into a multi-tier support model, with the first tier being largely unskilled workers who are trained to resolve issues using a simple script. If the first tier is unable to resolve an issue the issue is escalated to a more highly-skilled second tier. In some cases, there may be three or more tiers of support. Typically the third tier of support is the engineers or developers of the product. Call centres have their critics as well. Some critics argue that the work atmosphere in such an environment is de-humanising. Others point to the low rates of pay and restrictive working practices of some employers. There has been much controversy over such things as restricting the amount of lime that an employee can spend in the toilet. Furthermore, call centres have been the subject of complaints by-callers who find the staff often do not have enough skill or authority to resolve problems. Owing to the highly technological nature of the operations in such offices, the close monitoring of staff activities is easy and widespread. This can be argued to be beneficial, to enable the company to better plan the workload and time of its employees. Some people have argued that such close monitoring breaches human rights to privacy. Yet another argument is that close monitoring and measurement by quantitative metrics can be counterproductive in that it can lead to poor customer service and a poor image of the company. Many call centres in the UK have been built in areas that are depressed economically. This means that the companies get cheap land and labour, and can often benefit from grants to encourage them to improve employment in a given area. There has also been a trend to move call centres to India, where there is a large pool of cheap English-speaking labour. This phenomenon has led to media reports of poor telephone connections and operators with insufficient local knowledge to do their job. But, call centres in India may be more professionally managed than their counterparts elsewhere in the world. Whereas a typical call centre employee in the developed world may be a high school drop out, the typical employee in an Indian call centre is a graduate. Another popular call centre site is the Philippines. Owing to its abundant English speakers that are college graduates and Americanized when it comes to accent and culture. The Philippines was an American colony for almost 50 years. Filipinos are said to be the best outsourcing site outside North America since the accent is nearer to that of American Consumers. Canada is also a popular call centre site, with the relatively low Canadian dollar and low telecommunication rates. SITEL Corporation, which operates call centres in Ottawa and St. Catharines, Ontario is one-such company. Minacs is a good example of a Canadian owned and operated call centre that exploits the Canadian US dollar exchange rate to its advantage. So is also Clientlogic, operating around the world. Around the world, there are a number of professional organisations forming to develop and promote call centre best practice management and operation, to overcome the negative aspects of a call centre, particularly in India.

    Management of call centres involves balancing the requirements of cost effectiveness and service. Callers do not wish to wait in exorbitantly long queues until they can be helped and so management must provide sufficient staff and inbound capacity to ensure that the quality of service is maintained. However, stall costs generally form more than half the cost of running a call centre and so management must minimise the number of staff present. To perform this balancing act, call centre managers make use oi demand estimation, telecommunication forecasting and dimensioning techniques to determine the level of staff required at any time. Managers must take into account staff tea and lunch breaks and must determine the number of agents required on duty at any one time.

Forecasting results are vital in making management decisions in call centres. Forecasting methods rely on data acquired from various sources including historical data, trend data and so on. Forecasting methods must predict the traffic intensity within the call centre in quarter hour increments and these results must be converted to staffing rosters. Special attention must be paid to the busy hour, i.e. those two half hour periods during a day when traffic intensity is at its highest. Forecasting methods can also be used to pre-empt a situation where equipment needs to be upgraded as traffic intensity has exceeded the maximum capacity of the call centre.

There are many standard traffic measurements that can be performed on a call centre to determine its performance levels. However, the most important performance measures are:

- The average delay a caller may experience whilst waiting in a queue
- The mean conversation time, otherwise referred to as Average Talk Time (ATT)
- The mean dealing time, otherwise referred to as Average Handling Time (equal to ATT plus wrap up time)
- The percentage calls answered within a determined time frame (referred to as a Service Level or SL%)

There are many refinements to the generic call centre model. Each refinement helps increase the efficiency of the call centre thereby allowing management to make better decisions involving economy and service. The following list contains some examples of call centre refinements:

- Predictive dialling: Computer software attempts to predict the time taken for an agent to help a caller. The software begins dialling another caller before the agent has finished the previous call. This, because not every call will be connected (think of busy or not answered calls) and also because of the time it takes to set up the call (usually around 20 seconds before someone answers). Frequently, predictive dialers will dial more callers than there are agents, counting on the fact that not every line will be answered. When the line is answered and no agent is available, it is held in a retention queue for a short while. When still no agent has become available, the call is hung up and classified as a nuisance call. The next time the client is called an agent will be reserved for the caller.

- Multi-skilled staff: In any call centre, there will be members of staff that will be more skilled in areas than others. A Voice Response Unit can be used to allow the caller to select the reason for his call. Management software, called an Automatic Call Distributor, must then be used to route calls to the appropriate agent. Alternatively, it has been found that a mix of general and specialist agent creates a good balance.

- Queuing systems: The selection of a queuing system type is a very important decision in a call centre as it determines the level of quality of service. Queueing systems in call centres are usually described as M/M/N type queues where N is the number of agents. The preferred method of queuing is a FIFO (First In First Out) model, as it causes minimum delay to callers.

- Prioritisation of callers: Classification of callers according to priority is a very important refinement. Detecting emergency calls or callers that are reattempting to contact a call centre are examples of callers that could be given a higher priority.

- Automatic number identification: This allows agents to determine who is calling before they answer the call. Greeting a caller by name and obtaining his/her information in advance adds to the quality of service and helps decrease the conversation time.

There are many other issues that have to be planned for when managing a call centre. A few of these issues are listed here:

- Planning for failure of equipment
- Need for flexibility in meal-times
- Need for job variety and training
- Job exhaustion and stress
- Staff turnover

The various components in a call centre discussed in the previous sections are the generic form of a call centre. There are many variations on the model developed above. A few of the variations are listed here:112

- Remote agents: An alternative to housing all agents in a central facility is to use remote agents. These agents work from home and use a Basic Rate ISDN access line to communicate with a central computing platform. Remote agents are more cost effective as they do not have to travel to work, however the call centre must still cover the cost of the ISDN line.

- Temporary agents: Temporary agents are useful as they can be called upon if demand increases more rapidly than planned. They are offered a certain number of quarter hours a month. They are paid for the amount they actually work and the difference between the amount offered and the amount guaranteed is also paid. Managers must use forecasting methods to determine the number of hours offered so that the difference is minimised.

- Virtual call centres: Virtual calls centres are created using many smaller centres in different locations and connecting them to one another. The advantage of virtual call centres is that improve service levels, provide emergency backup and enable extended operating hours over isolated call centres. There are two methods used to route traffic around call centres namely, pre-delivery and post-delivery. Pre-delivery involves using an external switch to route the calls to the appropriate centre and post-delivery enables call centres to route a call they have received to another call centre.

Interaction centres: As call centres evolve and deal with more media than telephony alone, some have taken to the term, "interaction centre." E-mail, Web Callback and more-are gradually being added to the role.

SME Hotel Sector: Challenges of the Internet

ICT forces companies to find new ways to expand the markets in which they compete, to attract and retain customers by tailoring products and services to their needs, and to restructure their business strategy to gain competitive advantage. This affects every aspect of how business is conducted, changing internal processes as well as external relationships, modifying and restructuring entire economic sectors. The Internet and especially the web is one of the main driving forces for these new developments by providing new powerful tools and possibilities of doing business. For the accommodation sectors it is a perfect platform to bring information about their products to the customers all over the world, in a direct, cost minimizing, and time effective way. The hotel product is increasingly being sold electronically, and price has been identified as one of the key motivators for encouraging customers to purchase online. Both industry cost structure and the perishable nature of the product makes effective distribution particularly important in the hotel sector. A hotel room left unsold on any particular night cannot be stored and subsequently offered to the customer at a later date. Hotel companies use a variety of different distribution channels to help selling their product. While direct sales are most common, extensive use is normally made of a variety of intermediaries, including travel agents, tour operators, marketing consortia and representative companies. However, the importance of electronic distribution channels has grown significantly in recent years. The Internet has dramatically changed the way people communicate, search information, make decisions, and particularly the way in which they buy goods and services. In our work the Internet is regarded as a potential strategic tool tor competitive advantage for SME hotels in Austria. Based on our generic framework for competitive advantage in e-Business we identify several threats and opportunities for the hotel sector. These are evaluated by an expert survey with participants from the Austrian travel and tourism industry and a hotel survey in Austria

This study is based on a theoretical framework for the formulation and implementation of a competitive strategy by extending Michael Porter's Model of Competitive Advantage and using the Logics of Value concept, defined by Hans Akkermans. By analyzing how the technology and market developments (market logic and techno logic) influence the five competitive forces we define several threats for the industry. On the other hand, these two logics provide opportunities for value creation and value-capturing, which can be used to counteract the threats within the business logic of a specific SME hotel and to gain competitive advantage. The framework includes the following major steps:

In the first step we use the strategic concept of the five competitive forces to analyze an industry. This market-based view provides us with an overview of the development and threats caused by ICT within an industry, in particular by the Internet. To counteract these threats of the Internet and to achieve competitive advantage, a firm has to develop a strategy by using the opportunities of the Internet, This is the subject of the second step of our framework. The basic unit of competitive advantage is the discrete activity, which adds, creates, or captures value to a product or service. In this part we define several opportunities and activities a company can use to gain a competitive position. This is primarily based on the Logics of Value defined by Akkermans, The threats and opportunities are identified for the accommodation sector in Austria and evaluated by an expert survey. To get a broad picture of the use of the Internet as a strategic tool in the hotel sector we also conducted an online survey in the accommodation industry. Finally, the results will provide us with a detailed picture of the use of the Internet within the Austrian SME accommodation sector from the view of industry experts and the view of the hotels. By combining this data with our qualitative research about the opportunities of the Internet we will be able to offer recommendations for a competitive strategy.

In the first step, we chose an expert survey with industry experts to evaluate the identified threats and opportunities for the hotel sector in Austria. The expert survey was designed as an online survey. To achieve a high response rate, we decided to formulate only nine questions, as most of the contacted persons are in high management positions and very limited on time. The following topics for questions were chosen: identifying opportunities and threats for the tourism market players, identifying the threats for hotels caused by the Internet, identifying the opportunities for hotels provided by the Internet, and identifying the present use of the Internet. 110 questionnaires were sent by e-mail to managers in or associated with the travel sector, and 22 valid responses were returned. This represents a participation rate of 20 per cent. Regarding the management position within the organization about 50 per cent represent the business leader or head of the company, whereas the other 50 per cent can be allocated to middle management positions. The hotel survey within the accommodation sector in Austria was conducted after the expert survey. It was designed as an online survey containing 19 questions which can be categorized into the following topics: identifying the threats for hotels caused by the Internet, identifying the opportunities for hotels provided by the Internet, identifying the present use of the Internet, and enterprise information. As we wanted to address many SME facilities that are already using the Internet for their business, we chose the population of a DMS (destination management system). This database includes about 15,000 accommodation facilities from all possible categories in Austria. It can be seen as the largest available database also including SMEs like farm holiday or bed and breakfast facilities. This data was cleaned by removing duplicates and data sets with wrong or missing e-mail addresses. Finally, 7,500 questionnaires were sent by e-mail to accommodation facilities in Austria, and 297 valid responses were returned. This represents a participation rate ot 4 per cent. The response rate can be regarded as well distributed over the different types of facilities and over the provinces in Austria.

In this chapter we concentrate on the expert survey and compare the results with first findings from the hotel survey. Three questions regarding problems and advantages of the Internet for SME accommodation facilities were used in both surveys to allow a direct comparison of the results.

The first question of the expert survey investigates which market players of the travel and tourism industry are confronted with growing threats and which are provided with new opportunities by the Internet. The experts were asked to evaluate for each player the degree of opportunities or threats caused by the Internet. For each player they had to assign a number between 1 and 7, where 1 represents strong opportunities and 7 strong threats. This question aims to illustrate how the experts see the position of the different players of the travel and tourism industry in general, and in particular how the role of the hotel sector is seen compared to the other players. Eleven different players of the travel and tourism industry were identified for this question.

IT&T companies, hotel chains, and hotels with more than 50 beds are also very well rated with a score smaller than two. Hotels with less than 50 beds are rated with an average of 2.05, thus their opportunities are also seen as strong and above average. The only players which are confronted with stronger threats than opportunities are the travel agents, which received a rating of 4.59 from the experts. The situation for intermediaries such as travel agents, CRS/GDS, and tour operators is seen as more critical than for suppliers. It also illustrates that those players are rated within a larger 95 per cent confidence interval. For example, travel agents are rated between 3.8 and 5.3, which indicates that the experts are more indifferent about their future role compared to Airlines, which are rated between 1.2 and 1.8. The situation of the larger suppliers such as airlines and hotel chains can be seen as very strong, and IT&T companies as new players in the market have also good opportunities provided by the Internet. In general, an average rating of 2.39 sees the travel and tourism industry in a position of good opportunities.

To evaluate the threats caused by the Internet we used the threats identified by Gratzer to propose eight statements for the accommodation sector. The experts rated the threats with a general average of 3.4. All statements, except T_4, T_5 and T_6, were rated above average and regarded as relevant. Statement T_4 (x = 4.8) is seen as the least important threat for the hotel sector and is also rated within a large confidence interval (CI = 95%) between 3.8 and 5.8.

Threats caused by the Internet

Statement of Threats

T_1 The Internet reduces the entry barriers for potential new entrants, thus new hotels can appear on the market.

T_2 The reduced switching costs of buyers increase also the power of the buyers. Consumers can easily book at an other hotel.

T_3 The Internet is a possible instrument to bypass wholesale or retail channels.

T_4 The Internet offers new possibilities and instruments to meet customer needs by offering new products and services, which could substitute existing ones.

T_5 The Internet opens the distribution channels for new market players (reintermediation). Hotels have to cooperate with these new partners.

T_6 The Internet brings many more hotel into competition with one another by expanding geographic markets and reduced entry barriers, it can increase the pressure for price discounting.

T_7 The Internet offers new possibilities and instruments to meet customer needs thus the rivalry among existing companies within an industry can increase (e.g. if one hotel offers a virtual room, all others have to do so).

T_8 The customer can easily compare different prices and gain knowledge about products, thus the price becomes the most important decision criterion.

The statements T_3 (x = 2.5) and T_2 (x = 2.6) received the highest rating as possible threats. This indicates that the most important threats are seen in the changes of the retail and distribution channels. Hotels which are ignoring the new channels and possibilities are confronted with increasing threats. This is also indicated by the reduced switching costs of the buyers. By the use of the Internet the consumer can easily book at another hotel. Besides these more market view orientated statements we also formulated a question where the experts had to rate eight different problems the Internet causes to hotels in their daily work. The same question was evaluated within hotel survey. Out of these four problems the survey participants had to identify the four most important ones.

The three most important problems according to the experts are: faster reaction time, new personnel requirements, and additional workload. All three statements can be seen as an indication for organizational challenges within the hotel and the need for the company to adapt its daily work. The answers of the hotels were similar, they identify the same problems, except that new personnel requirements are not regarded as such important as stated by the experts. To evaluate the opportunities provided by the Internet we used the opportunities identified by Gratzer to propose nine statements (see Table 2). The average rating for the relevance of all mentioned opportunities is very high with a score of 2.3, which shows that all statements are identified as relevant. The lowest rating is x =2.8 for the statements O_9 and O_4.

Opportunities of the Internet

O_1 Using the Internet, hotels can use product bundling to provide new offers for their customers.

O_2 Using the Internet, hotels can provide special niche products for customers.

O_3 Hotels can use the Internet for personalized products and services.

O_4 The Internet offers possibilities for dynamic pricing.

O_5 The Internet offers new sales possibilities by using revenue sharing and affiliate programmes.

O_6 Using the Internet, hotels can contact their customers directly, intermediaries like travel agents are bypassed.

O_7 Using the Internet hotels can act as new intermediaries.

O_8 Using web and data mining technologies, hotels can capture additional information about their customers.

O_9 By conducting online surveys, hotels can capture additional information about their customers and potential customers.

As the most important opportunities the experts identified O_6 (x = 1.8) and O_2 (x = 1.9). O6 points to the importance of the Internet as a distribution channel and the possibility for hotels to bypass the existing ones. This is also underlined by the results of the first question, where the intermediaries are rated as those players who have less opportunities than the others. O_2 illustrates the chance for hotels to address niche products and the individual customer. We also included a question where the experts had to choose up to four advantages of the Internet for the hotel sector. The same question was evaluated within the hotel survey. The two most important advantages identified by the experts are: last minute bookings and lower distribution costs, these can be associated with an increased organizational level of a hotel. Also very important are activities and applications which support the more strategic part of a hotel work. These advantages are: new customers, higher utilization, and direct customer contact. The hotels rated the advantages in a very similar way but put more emphasis on higher utilization and direct customer contact than the experts.

To get a detailed picture of the present use of the Internet from the point of view of the experts we included a question with 12 different applications of the Internet, which hotels can use for their daily business. We asked the experts to identify those services which the hotels already use extensively for their business. There was no limitation of answers. Again, the same question was asked to the hotels within the hotel survey. The results show that the following services and applications of the Internet are seen as the most important ones: homepage, e-mail, and hotel reservation. Services like hotel booking, newsletter, and last minute offers are considered as only partly in use, whereas personalization activities, hotel surveys, or banner and hotel promotion are thought of not being used at all. The results of the hotel survey were very similar. E-mail is the most important service in use, followed by homepages and hotel reservation facilities. The largest difference can be found in product development, which is rated nearly twice as important than by the experts.

Thus, the purpose of this study is to explain the role of the Internet for hotels and similar accommodation facilities from the point of view of industry experts as well as of representatives from the accommodation industry. The experts identified the hotel sector as one of those players with large opportunities provided by the Internet. Hotels with more than 50 beds and hotel chains seem to be in a better position than SME hotels with less than 50 beds. In fact, larger hotels and hotel chains have always had a greater need of ICT and have already a higher level of ICT usage. However, the Internet can be seen as a powerful instrument for SME hotels to overcome this ICT disadvantage. By using the Internet, hotels can contact their customers directly, intermediaries like travel agents are bypassed, and SME hotels which have had no possibility to use distribution channels yet, can use the Internet as an additional and new channel. A nother opportunity can be seen by using the Internet to distribute niche products and address the individual customer. This is also evident as the experts have identified the changes of the retail and distribution channels as the most important threat for hotels and have rated the homepage as the second most important distribution channel for hotels in Austria. SME hotels cannot afford to ignore the importance of the Internet. It can be seen as one of the largest threats that SMEs failing to adapt their Internet presence and therefore being unavailable in the marketplace will be inaccessible to customers and intermediaries.

As identified by the experts as well as by the hotels, the most evident problems and threats for the hotels are: the faster reaction time and the additional workload. New personnel requirements are seen as a problem from the point of view of the experts, the hotels themselves are not aware of this problem. In general these are all organizational problems. The ability to handle these problems will be a very important success factor to gain competitive advantage by using the Internet. However, we identified also related advantages of using the Internet: last minute bookings and lower distribution costs, which are also associated with a more efficient organization of a hotel. These factors are indicated by the experts as well as by the hotels. We see it as an essential success factor for a hotel to create organizational structures, such as defining responsible persons or specific business processes for the introduction of new Internet technologies. The results of the surveys also illustrate that especially services like homepage, e-mail, and reservation activities are used extensively. More dynamic services like online booking, newsletters, or personalization tools are used less or not at all, up to now. In the next step of our research we will continue with the evaluation of the hotel survey and focus on the present use of the Internet to identify strengths and weaknesses. This will provide us with a broad picture of the awareness of hotels regarding the use of the Internet for their business activities. Finally, we will postulate possible recommendations for decision makers within this sector in Austria.

CONCEPT OF HOSPITALITY

- The concept of hospitality is the generous and cordial provision of services to the guests arriving at the various hospitality properties.
- These services, in the hotel industry, can include room accommodations, food and beverages, meeting facilities, reservations, information on hotel services, information on local attractions and so on.
- Hospitality is very subjective concept, and the degree of hospitality a guest perceives has implications for the overall final success of the hotel.
- Thus it is responsibility of the future professionals of the hospitality industry should develop a strong sense of responsibility for providing professional hospitality.
- Thus the delivery of hospitality efficiently to the guests is an essential responsibility of the hospitality professionals in order to satisfy the guests to the utmost extent.

IMPORTANCE OF HOSPITALITY

- Hospitality is very important consideration for both the guest and the hotel entrepreneur.
- Every guest expects and deserves hospitable treatment. Providing hospitality to meet guests' needs involves not only a positive attitude but a range of services that make the stay of the guest comfortable as well as enjoyable.
- If the market being served by the hotel is composed of business travelers, a hotel staff will find that their needs revolve around schedules and flexible delivery of hotel services.
- Thus the hotel restaurant must be well organized to be able to provide healthy and quick breakfast. The hotel should offer services

such as wake-up call, advanced telephone systems, fax facilities and computers. Besides, the hotel should also be able to arrange for the conference and meeting facilities.

- The success or failure in providing hospitality often determines the success or failure of the hotel. Thus capitalizing on opportunities to provide hospitality is essential. The failure to make the most of these changes directly affects the hotel's financial success.

- The hospitality deliverers know it very well that the guest who is not treated with hospitality will choose to do business with a competitor and may also influence others not to try the particular hotel.

- The entrepreneur who is aware of the competition realizes that negative advertising will severely affect the profit-and-loss statement.

- Thus hospitable treatment of guest must be more than just an option; it must be standard operating procedure. It is a concept that must be adopted as a corporate tenet and organized for effective delivery.

MANAGING THE DELIVERY OF HOSPITALITY

- It is not enough for the front office manager to decide that the members of the front office staff should provide good service and display hospitality to the guests.

- To provide satisfactory hospitality to all guests at all times, front office managers must develop and administer a service management program, which highlights a company's focus on meeting customers' needs and allows a hotel to achieve its financial goals.

- The management must work with full efforts behind the scene to develop a plan to ensure that the front office staffs deliver hospitality with a professional attitude.

- For example, management may decide to implement one or two specific, immediate changes on learning that a guest's needs have been overlooked.

- Thus the management should try to develop a program aimed at meeting the needs of a hotel's prime market – guests who continue to do business with the hotel – provides the foundation for long-term successful delivery of hospitality.

- Management's commitment to a service management program must be an integral to organization as effective market planning, cost-control programs, budgeting and human resource management.
- Thus service management program is the most visible responsibility because it affects all other objectives of the hotel.
- Service management ensures that there is a commitment to a long-range effort by appointing someone within the organization to be responsible for developing, organizing, and delivering it.
- The owner and general manager must make financial commitment to ensure the success of the program.
- An important component of the program is motivating employees to deliver hospitality on a continual basis through incentive programs.
- The goal of any lodging organization should be to extend the same degree of hospitality to guest who arrives on a busy day and also to a guest who arrives on a slag day.

CHAPTER – 2

SERVICE MANAGEMENT

THE SERVICE STRATEGY STATEMENT

- To produce an effective service management program, management must devise a service strategy statement, a formal recognition by management that the hotel will strive to deliver the products and services desired by the guest in a professional manner.
- Hence to accomplish this, the management must first identify the guest's needs.
- The staffs working at the entry-level position in a hotel are in direct contact with the guest and so they can anticipate the needs and demands of the guests in a better way.
- Thus the hotel management should use the observations of the entry-level position employees as a baseline for beginning to understand guests' needs while they are away from home, and thus the hotel management would be able to satisfy the guests in a better way.

- Thus, in addition to identifying generally what guests want, management should survey guests about the particular property to determine what services they expect and how they want these services to be delivered.
- The general manager may assign this task to the marketing and sales director, who may start reviewing and summarizing customer comment cards, which are usually held on file for six months to one year.
- A review of the areas in which the hotel has disappointed its guests, will provide a basis for determining where to begin a guest survey.
- The problem areas identified from this study are then used as the focus of a simple survey from.
- The survey may be administered by a member of the marketing and sales department at various times during the day.
- This information, as well as that collected from the comment cards, will give a general indication of what guest wants.

DEVELOPING THE SERVICE STRATEGY STATEMENT

Once the management has identified what guests want, it can develop a service strategy statement. The statement should include: -

- A commitment to make service from top-level ownership and management a top priority in the company.
- A commitment to develop and administer a service management program.
- A commitment to train employees to deliver service efficiently.
- A commitment of financial resources to develop incentives for the employees delivers the services who deliver the services.

These directives will serve as guidelines in the development of a service management program. More important, they force management to think of service as a long-range effort.

Here is one example of a service strategy statement: -

The owners of The Times Hotel, management, and staff will combine forces to establish a Service to Our Guests program, administered by management and delivered by staff. Delivery of service to our guests is crucial to the economic viability of our hotel. The owners of the hotel will provide financial support to the people who deliver hospitality on a daily basis.

MOMENTS OF TRUTH IN HOTEL SERVICE MANAGEMENT

- Central to the development of a guest service program is the management of "moments of truth", a circumstance in which a guest comes into contact with any aspect of the company, however remote, and thereby has an opportunity to form an impression.
- Every time the guest comes in contact with some aspect of the hotel, he or she judges its hospitality.
- Guests who are told by reservationists that they must ""take his room at his rate or stay elsewhere" will not feel that hospitality is the primary consideration at the particular hotel.
- The guest who is crammed into an elevator with half the housekeeping crew, their vacuum cleaners, and bins of soiled laundry will not feel welcomed. All these impressions make the guest feel that service at the particular is mismanaged.
- Whether a guest considers an event a moment of truth or barely notices, it is a cumulative review of the delivery of hospitality.
- Thus if the guest is to appreciate the service of a particular property, it is essential that these moments of truth be well managed. This challenge is not to be viewed as mission impossible but rather as an organized and concerned effort by owners, management, and employees.

EMPLOYEE BUY-IN CONCEPT

- All the sophisticated marketing programs, well organized sales promotions, outstanding architectural designs, and certified management staffs form only the backdrop for the delivery of hospitality.
- The frontline employee is the link in the service management program. He or she must deliver the service with a high level of consistency in order to satisfy the guest to the utmost extent.
- To have a high standard of service, it is necessary to create and maintain a motivating environment in which service people can find personal reasons for giving their best to the employees.
- Thus a consistent high level of service will be provided only by employees who are committed to the service management program.
- The hotel management has an important to play in order to foster this commitment in the employees.

- The following are some of the strategies that can adopted to motivate the staffs of a hotel: -

    a) Financial incentive programs should be implemented in order to motivate the staffs to give production.

    b) Employee stock ownership programs also provide an incentive for employees to realize financially the importance of delivering a consistently high level of hospitality.

    c) Other reward systems may include preferential treatment in scheduling shifts, longer vacations, and extra vacations, and extra holidays.

    d) Long range rewards may include promotion opportunities.

SCREENING EMPLOYEES WHO DELIVER HOSPITALITY

- It is an important job of the management to decide the employee character traits needed to provide hospitality while developing a service management program.
- When evaluating the candidates for the frontline service positions, interviews should be structured to screen out employees who are not able to deal with the demands of the guest service.
- Group discussions among the managerial staff will help to highlight the attributes of a person who will be able to deliver hospitality.
- These discussions should lead to a rather informal procedure for screening employees.
- Questions which determine whether candidates display maturity and self-esteem are clear, possess social graces and have a high level of tolerance for continued guest contact.
- The managers who are ware of what they are looking for in employees are better able to secure the right people for the right jobs.

TRAINING FOR HOSPITALITY MANAGEMENT

- Part of the service management program involves employee training to deliver hospitality.
- Just as managers discuss what they want in an employee, managers decide what must be done to convey hospitality to travelers who are away from home.

- This decision regarding this aspect is taken after performing a discussion and gathering valuable inputs from other employee.
- Using the guest cycle, the planning group determines what each frontline employee must do at each point to extend hospitality.
- It is extremely important to take care that the communications of hospitality must be identified, so that each employee can be properly trained to convey them.
- The key to make training program successful is to know what the management wants from the trainees to be able to do after the completion of the training program.
- An effective training process starts with performance analysis.
- The management must analyze the various jobs to be done in serving the customer well, and then spell out the knowledge, attitudes, and skills required of the person doing the jobs.

EVALUATING THE SERVICE MANAGEMENT PROGRAM

- All programs require methods for evaluating whether the program has successfully its achieved goal or not.
- Hence, as a step towards this direction, the hotel managements have developed a sound evaluation procedure on identifying the guest's moments of truth.
- The more research put into identifying the components of the guest service cycle for a specified hotel property.
- Specific desired behaviors of the guest as well as the employee can be observed and measured.
- Customer comment card is an important evaluation tool for the hotel as the hotel management comes to know the about the performance of the various operational departments of the hotel through the comments of the guests.
- Owners, managers, and employees who are committed to the service management program develop additional programs for determining the satisfaction level of the guests. One another method that can be used to obtain useful feedback from the guests is by having frontline staff, such as desk clerk, inquire about the guests' visit during check-out.
- A method of communicating the responses of the guests to the appropriate departments, which can rectify the errors or reward

the frontline employee, will complete the process of evaluating the success of a service management program.

FOLLOW THROUGH

- Vital to any service management program is the continued implementation of the program over time.
- In the hospitality industry, continued implementation of the program over time can very difficult.
- A hotel operates throughout the year and a large number of jobs are involved and performed in keeping it running smoothly and profitably.
- Management can begin a service management program with the best of its intentions, but too often it is dropped due to the day-to-day work operation pressures.
- The difference between a program and continuous commitment is management. Management is the key to implementing an effective guest service program.
- The commitment to hospitality is not a casual one; it requires constant attention, research, training and evaluation.
- Only with this commitment can a hotel ensure hospitality everyday for every guest.

COMPUTERS IN HOSPITALITY

Technology has become the basic requirement in the hospitality industry in the 21st century.

Hence every professional in the hospitality industry agrees on its increasing importance for the welfare and comfort of the guests primarily and then the employees at large and thus generating long run benefits, profits and goodwill at large.

Today, the hospitality industry is slowly being transformed through the application of advanced technological innovation, and this transformation is something more radical than mere improvements in machines.

Today, Information Technology or IT has become the essence of the hospitality industry.

Information Technology is usually associated with the electronic storage and retrieval of information the various operations of an organization .

Hospitality operatives are increasingly finding that new systems give them more skill, interest, responsibility and control over how they perform their jobs.

The organizations vision of a successful implementation of information technology can thus have a positive impact on the way in which managers perceive their role.

Thus, in the battle of hospitality entrepreneur against fate i.e. customer demand, his or her skills and techniques are like weapons, that they can use in a variety of way out of which information technology is just are of these weapons which becomes extremely important in the drive for a successful and profit maximizing establishment.

CAR RENTAL

- Car rental is a flourishing business throughout the world and is complementing the hotel industry by meeting the requirements of the guests demanding car rental during their arrival, stay and departure from the hotel.
- The car rental has also become a business in the metropolitan and other important cities of India.
- The important target markets for the car rental business are tourists, hotel guests as well as business and corporate travelers while traveling to other cities and countries.
- Nowadays, computers have fully automated the operations of the car rental services around many countries of the world.
- In the continents of Europe and America, the Information and Reservation systems such as **Amadeus**, **Sabre** and **Galileo** are used for car rental and information.
- The world's largest car rental company Hutch has also developed its own Information and Reservation system for providing car rental services to their potential clients.
- In India, the car rental service is at bud stage with a very few companies having fully automated car rental operations.
- *Wheels* is one of the frontline company in India solely dealing with the rental of vehicles and thus fulfilling care rental requirements for the tourists, guests and other business travelers.
- TCI, Thomas Cook, Graha Tours and Travels and other travel and tour operating agencies have transport divisions which are companies dealing with car rental services.

- The international Information and Reservation System such as Amadeus, Sabre and Galileo enables the instant confirmation of the car rental services in case of international booking through the computerized system.

- The computerized car rental services operating in a city domestically can have instant access about the free cars and taxis very quickly through their computerized network.

- The computerized car rental service companies maintain and updated inventory of all the available cars for rent and thus traces all the free cars and sends them for services to the customers efficiently and promptly.

- When international bookings are accepted by the IRS or travel agents, the bookings are routed to the sister concerns of the travel agencies through telephone, fax, e-mail etc. and thus the sister concern travel agencies in the host country receives international business and earns profit.

AIRLINES OPERATIONS

- The airlines industry has the maximum amount of the computerization in comparison to any other industry in the travel and tourism segment.

- The airlines industry uses the Global Distribution System to book air tickets for the various airline companies operating around the world.

- The Global Distribution system helps in achieving a better occupancy percentage in the flights and thus also plays a vital role in the marketing and popularity of the airline companies.
  - The first Information and Reservation System was developed in the country of U.S.A in the year 1970.
  - The IRS provided total information about the travel and tourism industry and also provided vital information about the airline industry.
  - The IRS also provided the facility of central reservation system for booking of the airline tickets in the flights of the various airline companies operating in U.S.A.

ADAVANTAGES OF IRS

- ♣♣ The IRS provided information about the flight schedules, flight timings, flight availability and also provided booking facility through the central reservation system.

- ♣♣ The IRS helps the airline companies to market and distribute their products to the target market and thus improve their efficiency and improve their market image.

- ♣♣ The IRS helps the travel agents to disseminate information travel segments and their demands, details of the flight schedules and bookings of airlines.

- ♣♣ The IRS also helps the various tour operators and departments of tourism of the various countries to gain information about making their services efficient and understand the customers and their requirements in better way.

- ♣♣ Many IRS are now providing information and reservation in various other product lines such as hotel, cruises, tours, car rentals and so on.

- o AMADEUS is a very popular Information and Reservation System founded in the year in 1987 by airline companies: Air France, Lufthansa, Iberia and SAS of which SAS has withdrawn its share holds.

- o AMADEUS is now known as the AMADEUS Global Distribution System and is electronic information and booking system providing worldwide distribution of the airline reservation.

- o AMADEUS displays flight information about 700 airline companies and accepts bookings for 430 airline companies.

- o AMADEUS now provides information and reservation facilities about accommodation in various world class hotels and car rental companies around the globe and also provides information about Rails, Tours and Cruises and their reservations.

- o AMADEUS has established more than 50 companies around the globe in partnership with the various domestic companies of the different countries.

- o These domestic companies are also called the National Marketing Companies of AMADEUS and these companies help to market the products of AMADEUS along with active customer service.

- o GALILEO is also an important Information and Reservation System which was commissioned in the year 1987 in England and was a joint venture of many airline companies.

- GALILEO was started with the purpose of providing information to the travel agents about the various airline companies and their reservation through the central reservation system.
- GALILEO also has collaboration with various domestic companies of different countries to distribute and sell their products to the customers and also provides information and reservations for hotels, cars, tours etc.
- SABRE opened in joint venture is perhaps the largest and most popular Information and Reservation System of U.S.A.
- SABRE provides central reservation system facility for airlines, hotels and car rental in the country of U.S.A but was not too much successful in Europe.

SERVICES OF COMPUTERS IN THE HOTEL INDUSTRY

RESERVATION

1) The computes are widely used in the reservation section of the front office departments of fully automated hotels around the world.
2) In, India also, in most of the well-known properties, the room reservation system has been fully automated through the use of computers.
3) Computers have replaced the traditional Whitney system of reservation which used to generate a lot of paperwork.
4) The computers used in the reservation sections maintain an updated inventory of the available rooms of the property for reservation.
5) The computers use various packages such as FIDELIO and SHAWMANN for the processing and storage of various important guest data regarding reservations.
6) The computers can be programmed to maintain an accurate data base for the various reservation requests of the guests and thus can store them for future retrieval
7) The introduction on the Local Area Network and Wide Area Network have led to the invent of central reservation system which is a reservation network of computers of a large number of hotels.
8) Thus, many chain hotels have their own central reservation system called the CRS which enables the guests to making room reservations for a hotel in one city from another city through the city booking offices of the hotel chain.

9) Many hotels have connected their central reservation system through the airline terminal to the Information and Reservation System (Global Distribution System) which provides them with worldwide bookings.

10) Thus, the main advantage of the computerized reservation system is that, one can have an accurate record of all the dates when rooms are available for sale and one can also keep a record of all the unsold and sold rooms of the hotel for a particular date.

FOOD AND BEVERAGE SERVICE

1) Computers are also widely used in the food and beverage service departments of large hotels for the smooth operation of the food and beverage service operations.

2) The computers are widely used in the preparation of guest bills for settlement and record, menu card preparation, inventory management and a variety of other food and beverage management functions.

3) Like room reservation, the computers are also used in the reservation or restaurant table for guests to have their meals and enjoy the dining experience in the food and beverage outlets.

4) The room service section of the food and beverage department also uses computers for keeping a track on the services. The room service order-taker takes down the order of the guest through telephone and then feeds the information in the computer which is connected to a printer or a monitor in the kitchen which instantaneously displays the order and thus the order is placed.

5) The food and beverage outlets use a Point-of-Sale software for the management of the entire operations of the outlets. The following are the main functional and vital files with the help of which the outlets work: -

a) Menu File: - The menu file records all the dishes in the menu of the outlet and gives a short description of them with their prices and taxes applicable.

b) Guest Receipt: - The guest receipt is an open data file and contains the guest names and items ordered by the guests. Each receipt will contain information about the guest name, name of the food and beverage outlet, the menu items ordered, individual price of the item, sub-total, taxes applicable and grand total.

c) Master File: - The master file will have important details about the employees of the Food and beverage outlet: the working hours of the employees, the amount of work performed by each employee and the wages earned by the employee.

    d) Inventory File: - The inventory file keeps a record of all the important products required For the operation of a food and beverage outlet and thus keeps a track on the purchase and utilization of the products.

6) The computers can also be used in the preparation of the various restaurant management reports which are used for reviewing the sale of the restaurant and thus they provide an insight to the eating trends and preferences of the guests, demands of the customers and also helps to predict the future manpower requirements of a restaurant.

ACCOUNTING AND BILLING

1) Computers are also used in the accounting of rooms, room services and restaurant services and also in other departments of the hotel.

2) The computers are used for storing the rates of the various rooms in the front office which are displayed when required.

3) The computers are also used to record the various charges which are incurred by the guests during the stay in the hotel.

4) The charges are posted in the guest folio and the folios are presented to the guests at the time of departure of the guest.

5) The computers are also used in the generation of various reports in the night audit process which is conducted in the front office regularly.

Food and Beverage Services - Organization

The food and beverage service is part of the service-oriented hospitality sector. It can be a part of a large hotel or tourism business and it can also be run as an independent business. The members of the F&B Services team are required to perform a wide range of tasks which include preparation for service, greeting the guests, taking their orders, settling the bills, and performing various other tasks after the guests leave.

Let us see the F&B services in hotels, structure of F&B department and ancillary services in a hotel.

Food and Beverage Services in Hotel

Most of the star-ranked hotels offer multiple F&B services in their hotels. They can be –

- Restaurant
- Lounge
- Coffee Shop
- Room Service
- Poolside Barbecue/Grill Service
- Banquet Service
- Bar
- Outside Catering Service

Structure of F&B Services Department

The F&B Services personnel are responsible to create the exact experience the guests wish for. The department consists of the following positions –

Food & Beverage Service Manager

The Food & Beverage Service Manager is responsible for –

- Ensuring profit margins are achieved in each financial period from each department of F&B service.
- Planning menus for various service areas in liaison with kitchen.
- Purchasing material and equipment for F&B Services department.

Assistant Food & Beverage Service Manager

The Assistant Food & Beverage Service Manager is aware of and is tuned to all the work the F&B Services Manager performs and carries out the same in the absence of his superior.

Restaurant Manager

The Restaurant Manager looks after the overall functioning of a restaurant. The responsibility of this staff member include –

- Managing the functions in the dining room
- Ordering material
- Stock-taking or inventory checking.
- Supervising, training, grooming, and evaluating the subordinates
- Preparing reports of staff and sales
- Managing budgets
- Handling daily sales and coordinating with cashiers

Room Service Manager

The Room Service Manager is responsible for –

- Selecting, training, encouraging, and evaluating all junior employees
- Ensuring that cultural values and core standards of F&B department/ establishment are met
- Controlling labor expenses through staffing, budgeting, and scheduling
- Handling guest complaints
- Providing special requests

Banquet Manager

The Banquet Manager is responsible for –

- Setting service standard for banquets
- Forecasting and allocating budgets for various types of events such as conferences, meetings, etc.
- Achieving food and beverage sales
- Controlling chinaware, cutlery, glassware, linen, and equipment
- Handling decorations and guest complaints
- Providing special requests

- Purchasing required stock by following appropriate requisition procedures
- Following up each function by receiving guest feedback and submitting it to F&B Manager
- Participating in departmental meetings
- Planning and pricing menu
- Training, grooming, and development of staff underneath

Bar Manager

The Bar Manager is responsible for –

- Forecasting the daily flow of customers
- Allocating right number of staff according to customer influx
- Managing and monitoring bar inventory from store to bar
- Tracking all types of drink sales
- Allocating cleaning and tendering tasks

Food Safety Supervisor (FSS)

A Food Safety Supervisor is a person who is trained to recognize and prevent risks associated with food handling in an F&B Services business. He holds an FSS certificate that needs to be no more than five years old. He is required in an F&B Services business so that he can train and supervise other staff about safe practices of handling food.

F&B Ancillary Departments

Food and Beverage department relies upon the support of the following departments –

Kitchen Stewarding

The Kitchen Stewarding department strives to ensure cleanliness, preparedness, and orderliness in the commercial kitchen so that the kitchen staff can work efficiently. It also ensures that all the tools and utensils required for a specific meal or cooking task are cleaned properly and are ready to go. The kitchen steward is a working link between the F&B Services and the commercial kitchen.

Dishwashing

The Dishwashing department is responsible for providing clean and dry supply of glassware, chinaware, and cutlery for bar, banquet, lounge, and restaurant service.

Laundry

The F&B department is highly reliable on laundry department or outsourced laundry services for timely supply of dry-cleaned and wrinkleless linen.

F&B Staff Attitudes and Competencies

Each member of the F&B department hierarchy needs to have the following traits and skills –

Knowledge

Awareness of one's responsibilities and roles, appropriate knowledge of food items, food and beverage pairing, etiquettes, and service styles is a great way to build confidence while serving the guests.

Appearance

It creates the first impression on the guests. The F&B staff members must maintain personal hygiene, cleanliness, and professional appearance while being on duty.

Attentiveness

Attentiveness is paying sincere attention to details, memorizing the guests' needs and fulfilling them timely with as much perfection as one can put in.

Body Language

The F&B Services staff needs to conduct themselves with very positive, energetic, and friendly gestures.

Effective Communication

It is very vital when it comes to talking with co-workers and guests. Clear and correct manner of communication using right language and tone can make the service workflow smooth. It can bring truly enhanced experience to the guests.

Punctuality

The F&B Services staff needs to know the value of time while serving the guests. Sincere time-keeping and sense of urgency helps to keep the service workflow smooth.

Honesty and Integrity

These two core values in any well-brought-up person are important for serving the guests in hospitality sector.

There are a number of service styles to be followed when it comes to how food and beverage should be served to the customers. The following are the most prominent styles –

Table Service

In this type of service, the guests enter the dining area and take seats. The waiter offers them water and menu card. The guests then place their order to the waiter. The table is covered in this service. It is grouped into the following types.

English or Family Service

Here, the host contributes actively in the service. The waiter brings food on platters, shows to the host for approval, and then places the platters on the tables. The host either makes food portions and serves the guests or allows the waiter to serve. To replenish the guests' plates, the waiter takes the platters around to serve or to let the guests help themselves. This is a common family service in specialty restaurants where customers spend more time on premise.

American or Plate Service

The food is served on guest's plate in the kitchen itself in predetermined portion. The accompaniments served with the food, the color, and the presentation are determined in the kitchen. The food plates are then brought to the guest. This service is commonly used in a coffee shop where service is required to be fast.

French Service

It is very personalized and private service. The food is taken in platters and casseroles and kept on the table of guests near their plates. The guests then help themselves. It is expensive and elaborate service commonly used in fine dining restaurants. This service has two variants –

- **Cart French Service** – The food is prepared and assembled at tableside. The guests select food from the cart while sitting at their tables and are later served from the right. It is offered for small groups of VIPs.

- **Banquet French Service** – The food is prepared in the kitchen. The servers serve food on each individual's plate from guest's left side. For replenishment, the servers keep the food platters in front of the guests.

Gueridon Service

In this service, partially cooked food from the kitchen is taken to the Gueridon Trolly for cooking it completely. This partial cooking is done beside the guest table for achieving a particular appearance and aroma of food, and for exhibiting showmanship. It also offers a complete view of food. The waiter needs to perform the role of cook partially and needs to be dexterous.

Silver Service

In this service, the food is presented on silver platters and casseroles. The table is set with sterling silverware. The food is portioned into silver platters in the kitchen itself. The platters are placed on the sideboard with burners or hot plates. At the time of serving, the waiter picks the platter from hot plate and presents it to the host for approval and serves each guest using a service spoon and fork.

Russian Service

It is identical to the Cart French service barring the servers place the food on the platters and serve it from the left side.

Assisted Service

Here, the guests enter the dining area, collect their plates, and go to buffet counters and help themselves. The guests may partially get service at the table or replenish their own plates themselves.

Buffet Service

It this type of service, the guests get plates from the stack and goes to buffet counter where food is kept in large casseroles and platters with burners. The guests can serve themselves or can request the server behind the buffet table to serve. In **sit-down buffet** restaurants, the tables are arranged with crockery and cutlery where guests can sit and eat, and then replenish their plates.

Self Service

In this type of service, the guests enter the dining area and select food items. They pay for coupons of respective food items. They go to food counter and give the coupons to avail the chosen food. The guests are required to take their own plates to the table and eat.

Cafeteria Service

This service exists in industrial canteens, hostels, and cafeterias. The menu and the space is limited; the cutlery is handed over to the guests. The tables are not covered. Sometimes high chairs are provided to eat food at narrow tables. It is a quick service.

Single Point Service

In this type of service, the guest orders, pays for his order and gets served all at a single point. There may be may not be any dining area or seats. The following are the different methods of Single Point Service.

Food Court

This is an array of autonomous counters at which the customers can order, eat, or buy from a number of different counters and eat in adjacent eating area.

Kiosks

The customer enters the choice and amount of money physically and the machine dispenses what customer demanded accurately.

Take Away

Customer orders and avails food and beverage from a single counter and consumes it off the premises.

Vending

The customer can get food or beverage service by means of automatic machines. The vending machines are installed in industrial canteens, shopping centers, and airports.

Special Service

It is called special service because it provides food and beverage at the places which are not meant for food & beverage service. The following are the different methods of special service.

Grill Room Service

In this type of service, various vegetables and meats are displayed for better view and choice. The counter is decorated with great aesthetics, and the guest can select meat or vegetable of choice. The guest then takes a seat and is served cooked food with accompaniments.

Tray Service

Method of service of whole or part of meal on tray to customer in situ, such as hospitals, aircraft, or railway catering.

Trolley/Gueridon Service

Food is cooked, finished or presented to the guest at a table, from a moveable trolley. For example, food served on trollies for office workers or in aircrafts and trains.

Home Delivery

Food delivered to a customer's home or place of work. For example, home delivery of pizza or Meals on Wheels.

Lounge Service

Service of variety of foods and beverages in lounge area of a hotel or independent place.

Room Service

Here food is served to guests in their allotted rooms in hotels. Small orders are served in trays. Major meals are taken to the room on trolleys. The guest places his order with the room service order taker.

The waiter receives the order and transmits the same to the kitchen. Meanwhile, he prepares his tray or trolley. He then goes to the cashier to prepare and take the bill. He then takes the bill along with the food order for the guests' signature or payment. Usually clearance of soiled dishes from the room is done after half an hour or an hour. However, the guest can telephone Room Service for the clearance as and when he has finished with the meal.

Today, numerous types of food and beverage service outlets have come up in the market. They offer a wide range of food and beverage services that the customers can avail. The extent of service depends upon the type of service outlet. They include drive-through service of fast food where the customers can purchase their favorite food without having to leave their cars and pick-up points where food is delivered in minutes. There are also some elite class fine dining outlets which exhibit classy articles in the house and provide elaborate food services.

Here are some famous types of food and beverage outlets –

Outlet	Menu	Ambience	Service
Airport Lounges	Wide menu for breakfast, lunch, and dinner with hot and cold beverages, salads, main meals, and desserts.	Soft instrumental music, soft lights, formal ambience, all appealing for having meals at leisure and resting gracefully at the airport	Self or Assisted service provided 24X7, round the clock. The traveler selects food and beverage of choice, and takes to the table himself.
Bars	Wide menu of soft drinks, alcoholic beverages, and light snacks.	Informal, relaxed atmosphere, energetic music, colorful flashy lights.	Push-low seating, speedy service of cocktails, mocktails, and snacks.
Cafeterias	Short dining menu with less food options. Follows cyclic meal plan.	Attached to educational institutes or industrial organizations	Self or assisted, pre-plated, low priced service.
Coffee Shops	Short menu with hot and cold beverages, snacks, and light meals.	Informal ambience with light music and moderate lighting.	Quick and mid-priced service for high customer turnover.
Discotheque/ Nightclubs	Menu with snacks and beverages.	Strobe lights, laser lights, dance floor, lively music, informal and energetic atmosphere.	Entry permission for couples or members on charge, assisted service.

Family/ Casual Dining Restaurants	Elaborate menu of single or multiple cuisines which may change according to the operating hours.	Modestly furnished, Casual atmosphere.	Assisted, mid-priced service.
Fast Food Outlets	Limited menu of hot and Cold beverages with easily prepared and fast meals cooked in advance and kept warm.	Catchy trendy colored furniture, lights, and music.	Speedy service, minimum table service. The food is prepared in the kitchen, placed in the trays, and passed to the person at the counter, who then delivers to the customer. The customer picks up the trays and consumes it on premise.
Food Courts	Multi cuisine menu.	Multi-cuisine food outlets are located around modestly kept central dining area.	Speedy service with minimum personal attention. The customers pick up food and beverages of their choice from multiple outlets around and sit in the central dining area to consume.

Grill Rooms	Grilled meat or sea food with alcoholic/ non-alcoholic beverages.	Attached to star hotels, gardens, or independent, may have open kitchen. Eye-catching counters.	According to hotel policies.
Poolside Barbeque	Roasted meats, crunchy vegetables, and seafood with wines and beer.	Located near swimming pools, Informal, relaxed atmosphere, energetic music.	Self/assisted service.
Pubs	Mostly alcoholic menu with snacks.	Informal and social ambience with less lighting and more chatting.	Push-low seating, self, or assisted service.
Specialty/ Ethnic Restaurants	Specific menus such as Chinese, Italian, Indian, Thai, or Mexican.	Follows specific theme. Interior Decoration is in line with the theme.	Uniform of the service staff, linen, and service ware are according to the theme and from the country where the food originates.
Take-away Counters	Limited or elaborate menu of food and beverages.	Frontend counter for selling is attached to the pantry.	Pickup service where customer places order, waits till it is completed, and picks the food and beverages to consume them off-premise.

Themed Restaurant	Limited menu that is based on the theme.	Architecture, lighting, and music induce the feel of the theme. Mostly informal ambience.	American/ Assisted service.
Vending Machines	Pre-packaged chips, portioned foods, canned beverages.	Located in high labor cost and limited space areas such as transport hubs.	Complete self-service.

General Layout of F&B Outlets

Appropriate architecture of F&B outlet makes it prepare, present, and serve in optimum way and increase productivity. These are few basic considerations for various sections of F&B outlets –

Kitchen

It is farthest from the customers.

Store

It has large fridges, cupboards with multiple shelves, and lockers. It is attached to the kitchen.

Pantry

It is being the area where food or beverage is prepared ready to serve, it is located between the dining area and the kitchen.

Restrooms

There are two different schools of thought for location of restrooms – some experts consider that the restrooms must be near the entrance and some think that it should be isolated from entrance or dining area.

General Considerations for F&B Services Layout

While designing an F&B outlet, one needs to consider every factor that contributes to the smooth running of operations right from food preparation, cooking, dish presentation, serving, and all allied tasks.

While designing commercial F&B outlets, the following points are important –

- Target customer segment (Youth/Men/Women/All).
- Type of food (Light Food/Fast Food/Fine Dining).
- Manner of food production (Cooking/Grilling/Boiling/Baking/Steaming).

- Type of food distribution (On/Off Premise).
- Availability of carpet area.
- Number of staff required.

The kitchen is designed not to be directly visible. The chef cannot directly communicate to the guests. The guest tables and chairs are placed away from kitchen.

Food and Beverage Service operations involve a multitude of activities which engage the staff right from purchasing raw material, preparing food and beverage, keeping the inventory of material, maintaining service quality continuously, managing various catered events, and most importantly, analyzing the business outcomes to decide future policies.

Let us look into the operations involved in F&B service –

Product Cycle in F&B Service

The purchasing department in F&B Services is responsible for purchasing, storing, and issuing the supply of raw food items, canned/bottled beverages, and equipment. The following is a typical product purchasing cycle –

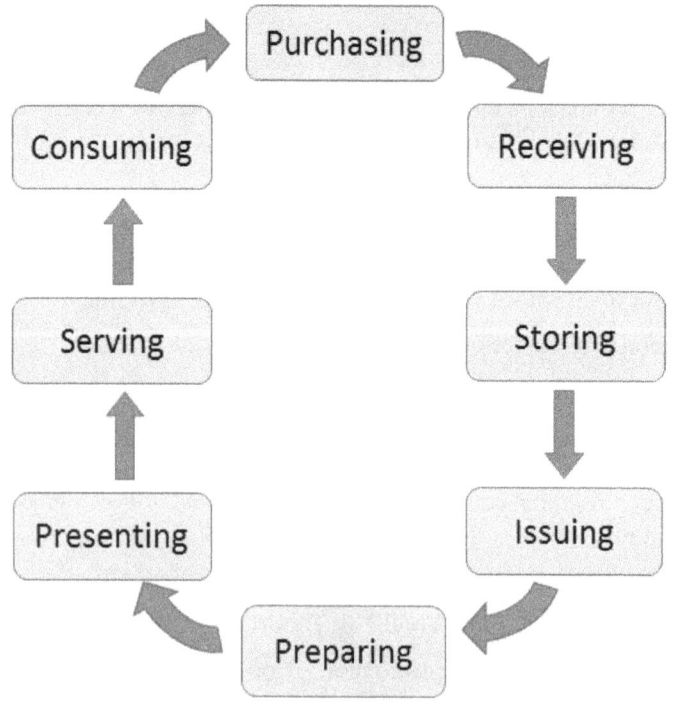

The purchasing department works with accounts department to keep the information on allocated budget and balance budget.

The following factors influence purchasing –
- Size of F&B Organization
- Location of F&B Organization
- Availability and Size of Storage Space
- Organization Budget and Policies
- Availability of the commodity due to season

Purchasing Product

The purchaser is responsible for purchasing a product. He studies the market, and analyzes and selects suppliers, wholesalers, and the contemporary market prices. He then liaisons with suppliers and wholesalers to get good material at fair price and purchases the required commodities by following appropriate purchase procedures.

Receiving the Product

The receiver receives the products from the suppliers. He checks the product for right quality and quantity. He deals with the delivery personnel from the supplier's end and signs on the related receipts.

Storing and Issuing the Product

The store men carry out the task of storing received supply and issuing it to respective departments. They update the stock database, and manage old and new material in the stock. They also keep record of stock to the latest date.

Preparing and Presenting an F&B Product

This includes preparation of various food items and fresh beverages. The cooks prepare various foods and the bar tenders prepare cold beverages such as mocktails and cocktails. They also make the dish most presentable by arranging food on platter and decorating it in an attractive manner. The beverages are also decorated by using fruit slices, decorating the glasses, sippers, and stirrers.

Consuming the F&B Product

This part is played by the guests. At the service end, the respective staff takes inventory of the consumed and balanced stock of food and beverages and keeps it updated to latest figures.

Maintaining Food and Beverage Standards

It is very vital for an F&B Services organization or an F&B department in a large hotel to keep their standards of food and beverage high. If the quality of food and beverage along with the best service is what the guests liked, then the chances of the guests coming repeatedly and singing praises of what they received are high.

Food and Beverage Standards

Any food and beverage service business has a great responsibility of serving hygienic, safe, clean, and fresh food. The customers also rightfully question if the food or beverage they consume at the F&B Services outlet is healthy, safe, and fresh.

For ensuring food safety, a system named Hazard Analysis and Critical Control Points (HACCP) in Europe works to identify Critical Control Points (CCP) for the presence of physical, chemical, and bacterial hazards to food. HACCP has set guidelines and principles on producing healthy and safe food. It also enables food and beverage businesses to adhere to consistent safety and quality of food production.

In India, Food Safety and Standards Authority (FSSA) works towards setting standards for safe and hygienic food. In USA, Food Safety and Inspection Service (FSIS) is responsible for the safety of meat, poultry, and processed egg products. Also, the Food and Drug Administration (FDA) is responsible for virtually all other foods.

Managing Buffets, Banquets, and Catered Events

Before planning and executing buffets, banquets, or catered events, the respective managers and supervisors need to consider the following factors −

Type of Event

It can be formal such as seminars, meetings, or conference, or informal such as a wedding reception, birthday party, employee outing, and alike.

Involvement of Various Persons

The participants such as decorating staff, planning staff such as managers, serving staff, supervising staff, whole sellers, and the guests.

Event Requirements

It is important to know the date and time of event, the number of expected guests, dance floor, audio or projector systems, or any special requirement demanded by the guests before planning the event.

Decors

It includes flowers, table arrangement, center-pieces, candles, artificial fountains/waterfalls, decorative art pieces, plants and pots; for both formal and informal occasions with the involvement of décor artists. The display pieces may be carved, baked, or assembled; made of edible or non-edible substances according to the laid standards. The decoration needs to go in pair with the theme of the banquet, buffet, or some event.

Menu

According to the time of event, it can include starters, salads, breads, main courses (meats, poultry, or sea food), desserts (fruits, pastries, or frozen desserts), beverages, accompaniments, and garnishes according to the establishment standards. It must be hygienic, in-line with the occasion, and meeting the F&B Services establishment standards.

Serving Equipment

Depending upon the requirement of guests and serving style, it can include silverware, platters, table linens, and other required serving equipment. It also includes size and shape of tables and chairs.

Serving Norms

According to establishment norms, serving right food at right temperature, replenishing food platters timely, keeping the overall display neat and attractive, storing food and managing beverage consumption after service, cleaning buffet or banquet area, restoring plates, cutlery, Guerion trollies, and glassware after completion of service.

The decision making responsibility in an F&B establishment rests with the managers. They have full access to the numbers, data, reports, and trends of the market as well as knowledge of F&B establishments.

F&B Services Analysis

The F&B services managers need to conduct **financial analysis** and **quality analysis**.

Financial Analysis is carried out in three steps –

Setting expectations (BUDGET)

The managers study current and future market trends and forecast expenses. Budgets are prepared based on managers' inputs.

Evaluating actual situation (INCOME STATEMENT)

The managers also keep a keen eye on present situation in which F&B Services is functioning. They need to consider **fixed costs** such as rents and property taxes, and **variable costs** such as material, advertisement, and music and entertainment costs.

Analyzing the difference (PROFIT/LOSS)

They come up with the difference and find out the reasons and apply the required policies.

The **Quality Analysis** needs to consider the following factors while providing the food product or service. Some of these factors are –

- Evaluating ongoing product analysis checklist that includes doneness, aroma and taste of the ready dish, garnish, color, appearance, presentation, serving portion, and alike.
- Evaluating the food or beverage product for safety against consumption.
- Evaluating weekly review of product deviation that includes date, product name, problem, solutions, and recommendation.

F&B Services Decision Making

It includes coming up with corrective actions in case of certain unpleasant results. The managers make decisions after going through the following steps –

- Identifying problems
- Identifying reason
- Determining a number of solutions
- Selecting a best solution
- Applying the solution
- Evaluating the solution

For example, the response for chilled cucumber soup is declining for the past four months.

- **Identify problems** – Menu problem? Taste issue? Price issue? Serving quantity or quality issue?
- **Identify reason** – Soup is outstanding on quality, portion of service, and taste marks. But it is Winter and guests are preferring hot soups than the chilled ones though it is on the lunch menu.
- **Solutions** – Can a hot variant of the same soup be developed? Can the soup be replaced by a preferred alternative?

- **Best solution** – Shift chilled cucumber soup to summer-time menus and bring in a new hot soup or a variant of one of the present soups that will potentially rule the guests' taste buds.

Food and beverages form an integral part of the human culture. Ever since human culture started evolving, food and beverages preparation also went on finding new ways. Today, every country flaunts a different line of food and beverages prepared in authentic culinary ways.

Over the past several years, various food and beverages have been developed using local crops, meats, fruits, and vegetables, and trying different recipes with them. This manner of development contributed in the authenticity of the food and beverages to a great extent.

What is Menu?

It is a detailed list of food and beverage offerings with their respective prices. It is prepared by a food and beverage service businesses to keep the customers informed about the availability of various F&B items.

A good menu must –

- Present clear, unambiguous information.
- Adhere to food safety and nutrition policies of the business.
- Meet or outstrip guests' expectations.
- Meet the quality standards of the business.
- Be truthful in describing the taste and preparations.
- Be strictly going with the production and service facilities of the business.

Restaurant Menu Preparation

The restaurant menu should be planned well by considering various aspects of the food outlet. There are myriad menus available right from breakfast, lunch, small bites, up to dinner. The following information is gathered before planning food and beverage menu for a commercial kitchen.

- What kind of food outlet is it? (Vintage, Contemporary, Modern, Theme, Bar, and more)
- What is the name of the outlet?
- What is the expanse of food items, their accompaniments, and beverages the owner wishes to keep?
- Which information needs elaboration for food and beverages?
- What tone of language is required? (formal/informal)

- What types of names and category headings would best suit for the food and beverage items?
- What design, images, colors, and typeface would look best for the menu?
- Are the graphic details relevant to the food outlet theme?
- How large should the menu be on paper?

These days, numerous apps such as MenuPro, FineDine, MenuExpress, InnMenu, and more are readily available to create catchy and engaging menus. A good menu design is a treat for eyes that drive the guests to place orders.

Depending upon the expanse of physical outlet and service, and the variety of food and beverages it offers, the menu design and details change.

Menu Planning

This is the selection of menu in advance for an upcoming event. Menu planning plays an important role in customer satisfaction.

Menu planning is beneficial in the following areas –

- Purchasing of essential material in advance.
- Pricing of the food.
- Guiding the food preparation.
- Evaluating the dietary needs.
- Evaluating the food in terms of necessary improvements.

The menu must be planned such that it goes well with the theme of the F&B outlet and it must be a good bargain for food price and dietary value.

There are various cuisines around the world. Each cuisine involves a lot of preparation. The following most famous ethnic menus are prepared in various cuisines around the world

Indian Food Menu

Indian food is perhaps as diverse as its culture and offers a lot more than curries and gravies. It balances all tastes — savory, sweet, salty, and sour. Indian food broadly goes according to the regions where it originates such as Northern, Southern, Western, and Eastern. Within regions it is varied according to states such as Kashmiri, Punjabi, Gujarati, Marathi, Keralite, Bengali, and so on. **It is an authentic combination of the base food paired with aromatic herbs nuts, and spices.**

It includes various appetizers, snacks and their accompaniments, veg and non-veg stews, various types of flat breads, plain or spicy lentils, rice preparations, sea-food, street food, and sweets made of milk products and nuts.

Indian food is eaten using one's clean fingers because that way, the flatbreads are easy to portion. The spoons and forks are used for having snacks, curries, stews, rice, curds, or sweets when the need arises. Authentic Indian food is generally served in copper or brass bowls and plates or you can have it on fresh banana leaves or *Patravali* (Plates made of dried leaves), which help to save efforts of cleaning and disposing.

A few popular Indian foods are –

- **Poh**a (beaten rice soaked and cooked by adding chopped vegetables and cilantro)
- **Aloo Bonda** (Boiled, mashed, and flavored potatoes enwrapped with lentil flour and deep fried)
- **Kadhai Panner** (Savory cubes of cottage cheese in thick tangy curry or gravy)
- **Veg Kolhapuri** (Wholesome vegetables cooked in spicy red gravy)
- **Rajma** (Black beans cooked in spicy gravy)
- **Biryani** (Aromatic and flavored rice dish cooked with vegetables or meat)
- **Sarson-da-saag** (Mustard leaves cooked with chili, garlic, and mustard oil)
- **Jalebi** (Coils of flour batter deep fried and dipped in sugar syrup)
- **Gulab Jamun** (Deep fried balls of milk powder and flour soaked into sugar syrup)

French Food Menu

France boasts of a wide range of cuisines. The cuisines follow authentic traditional cooking practices. French food caters to the preparation of appetizers, salads, soups, stews, side and main dishes, and desserts. A large variety of classic food is prepared using red and white meats. Recipes have evolved with seafood, fruits, cheeses, vegetables, pastries, and chocolates using authentic sauces and dressings.

The following are some traditional French dishes are –

- **Soupe a l'oignon** (Onion soup in meat stock)
- **Petits Pates a la Sage** (Little pies of sage)
- **Ratatouille** (Traditional vegetable stew)
- **Coq au vin** (Rooster in wine)

Italian Food Menu

Italian food boasts of classically prepared pizza bases baked with savoury toppings of vegetables, meat, and cheese. It also includes a wide range of pastas of various shapes and sizes cooked and served with authentic Italian accompaniments and sauces.

The local customs of baking and cooking provide a large array of soups, salads, snacks, meals, and desserts from Italian cuisine. The food is often accompanied with beverages such as wine, champagnes, or other similar drinks.

The following are some popular dishes in Italian cuisine –

- **Bellini** (a cocktail made with white peach puree and sparkling wine.)
- **Caprese Salad**
- **Cacciuco** (Seafood stew)
- **Risotto Alla Milanese** (Saffron Rice)
- **Arancini Veneziani** (Venetian Rice Fritters)
- **Braciola** (Italian Beef Rolls in Tomato Sauce)
- **Spinach and Mushroom Lasagna** (Baked sheets of flour separated by stew and cheese)

Chinese Food Menu

They say, Chinese food is the tastiest in the world. It includes soups, snacks, and meals prepared with rice, noodles, vegetables, meats, seafood, sauces, and seasonings. The stir frying manner of cooking brings crunchiness, texture, and adds a great flavor to various Chinese dishes.

Chinese food is prepared with crunchy or leafy vegetables, bean sprouts, a variety of mushrooms, bamboo shoots, tofu (soybean curds), and spices such as chilies, ginger, Chinese celery, and garlic. The food is consumed using traditional chopsticks and spoons. The table setting displays porcelain bowls and spoons for soup, a large bowl for food kept on the flat plate underneath, Rice bowl, and a pair of chopsticks with resting stand.

The following are some traditional Chinese dishes –

- **Gong Bao Chicken** (Diced chicken cooked with dried chili and fried peanuts).
- **Ma Po Tofu** (Tofu cubes cooked with pepper powder, ground beef, and green onions).
- **Wontons** (Triangles of flour added in soup).
- **Dumplings** (Small dough disks filled with minced meat or spicy chopped vegetables, closed, and steamed).
- **Spring Rolls** (fried cylindrical rolls that enwrap minced meat or vegetables).
- **Chow Mein** (Cooked and stir fried vegetables in savory sauce).

Chinese food includes a cup of tea as beverage. No aerated drinks are served as part of authentic Chinese meal. Desserts are not commonly consumed in Chinese cuisine except on special occasions. The meal is generally completed with fruits.

Thai Food Menu

Thai food is popular for the aroma it brings with the addition of lemongrass, lemon leaves, galangal, chili, and aromatic herbs. The base food is vegetables, meats, eggs, sauces, noodles, and rice. A complete Thai meal comprises of snacks, salads, soups, one-dish meals, and desserts. It makes a blend of great taste and treat for eyes too.

As per the traditional customs, the soups are enjoyed along with rice and noodles; not before. The rice or noodles are topped with the toppings of choice and consumed with spoon. Some popular Thai dishes are –

- **Tom Yam Goong** (Jumbo prawns in savory hot and spicy sauce)
- **Pad Thai** (Noodles with tofu, sprouts, fried onion, chili sauce, and finely powdered peanuts)
- **Kuay Tiew** (Noodles served in vegetables and meat broth)
- **Gai Med Ma Moung** (Chicken in soy sauce, garlic, honey, and cashew nuts)

- **Kao Phad** (Fried rice)
- **Massaman Curry** (Meat and potato cooked in cinnamon flavored curry)

Mexican Food Menu

Mexican line of food is famous for spicy and tangy taste. It includes salads, snacks, one-dish meals, elaborate meals, and desserts.

The basic food items in Mexican cuisine are –

- **Tortillas** (Corn flour or wheat flour disks)
- **Fajitas** (Grilled meat on tortilla)
- **Tacos** (Small tortilla partially enwrapping the filling)
- **Quesadillas** (Wheat or corn tortilla filled with cheese and meat or vegetables)
- **Nachos** (A Texan-Mexican or Tex-Mex snack with savory flavored tortilla chips)
- **Enchiladas** (Corn tortillas rolled around a filling of cooked meat, seafood, beans, or vegetables and covered with a chili pepper sauce and cheese)
- **Empanadas** (Baked or fried stuffed bread or pastry)

Corn, black beans, native fruits and vegetables, herbs, and meats are integral ingredients of Mexican food. A few popular Mexican dishes are –

- Chicken-mango-jalapeno salad
- Mango-pineapple salsa
- Prawn fajita with avocado cream
- Mexican chicken stew
- Grilled chicken nacho
- The courses of meal around the world vary in number from as small as just one to as wide as 17, in case of a traditional French meal. The courses are divided according to what food one eats. There are different food profiles according to the country's culture and customs. Generally, there are at least three courses of a meal –
- Starter

- In this course, a welcoming appetizer that induces hunger is given to the guests. Also, the guests can prefer soups accompanied with the bite-size savory snacks as side orders in this course.
- Main Course
- During this course, main dishes with vegetables or meats accompanied with rice and breads are served. In some cultures, such as Indian, the main dish is accompanied with salads.
- Dessert
- This course signals the end of meal and is usually had with a cup of coffee.
- Salads form an important part of diet in France. A typical French meal has an addition of Salad Course. It is often accompanied by other courses such as Fish Course and Cheese Course. There are cultures where people prefer to take one dish meal with no elaborate and distinguished courses of food.
- Broad Types of Menus
- Depending upon what and how the food is made available to the guests, there are following broad menu types –
- Table D'hote Menu
- Table D'hote is a menu where the meal is combined with a number of food options from each course. **The guests can make their choice and order for a fixed price**. Irrespective of what the guest chooses or declines, the price remains the same. Hence, it may also be called *prix fixe* or *fixed price* menu. Banquet menus, children's menus, and occasion menus cater to special occasions and are offered at a set price.
- A la carte Menu
- A la carte is a multi-course or multi-category menu that comes with appetizers, starters, sea-food, meats, side dishes, beverages, and alike. Each dish is offered at a separate price. The guest can choose individual dishes to make own meal package.
- Static Menu

- In this menu, the typical types of meals are served yearlong with an occasional change on some special days.
- Cyclic Menu
- Cycle menu includes different meals offered on different days of a week. The cafeterias at educational institutes and otherwise use this menu which they can repeat after a week or a month. Serving a feast on Sunday, offering special variants of chicken on Fridays can add to the cyclic menu.
- Let us now look at a few other menus which boost your platter and the F & B Services.
- Dessert Menu
- This menu displays puddings, cakes, tarts, ice creams, smoothies, fondues, sundaes, sweet pies, and ice creams and frozen yogurts along with their respective prices.
- **Frozen Desserts** – They are usually popular with people from all ages and walks of life. They are always served chilled. The following are some mouthwatering frozen desserts are –
- **Ice Cream/Gelato (Italian for ice-cream)** – They are primarily same with just a little difference in composition of milk, custard, water, and eggs. In India, frozen desserts are prepared with thick full cream milk and fruit pulp or crushed nuts and saffron. It is popularly known as '*Kulfi*'. Kulfi is served on stick or in terracotta pot called '*Matka*'.
- **Sorbet** – It is a frozen dessert made of fruit juices, dessert wines, and ice shaves. It is flavored by a variety of edible food colors and essences. In contrast to ice cream, frozen dessert appears icier than milky.
- **Frozen Yogurt** – It is made by freezing flavored yogurt. It also contains less fat, sugar, and thus less calories as compared to ice creams.
- Beverage Menu
- This menu includes variants of tea and coffee, hot chocolate, juices, milkshakes, mocktails, and so on. The wine menu includes wines, beers, liquors, types of water, cocktails, and spirits with their respective serving quantities and prices.

- Beverage is any liquid consumed by humans for quenching thirst, or merely for pleasure. Beverages come in various types –
- Non-Alcoholic Beverages
- There are two types of non-alcoholic beverages.
- Hot Beverages
- These are served hot. Hot beverages typically include tea, masala tea (spiced tea), milk, hot chocolate, and variants of coffee such as expresso, latte, and cappuccino.

Cold Beverages

These are served and consumed while chilled. Cold beverages include juices, mocktails, coolers, cold versions of tea and coffee, milkshakes, carbonated drinks, mocktails, and sherbets. The following beverages are famous in countries like India –

- **Buttermilk** with a dash of powdered cumin seeds and salt.
- *Aam Panna*, a sweet and sour raw mango juice with a dash of cardamom in it.
- Tender coconut water locally called *Nariyal-Pani*.
- *Sol Kadhi*, thin coconut milk flavored with Kokum and ginger-garlic-chili paste.

There are a few cold beverages which come as cocktails and are prepared using alcohol.

Alcoholic Beverages

These are served cold. Alcoholic beverages are intoxicating and contain *ethanol*, commonly known as alcohol. Such beverages need to undergo fermentation and distillation to generate alcohol contents. The percentage of alcohol varies in the range of 0.5% to 95% depending upon the methods of fermentation and distillation.

- Wine, Cider, Perry, and Champaign are **fermented** alcohols.
- Beer, ale, and lager are **fermented and brewed** alcohols.
- Gin, Vodka, Whisky, Rum, Brandy, and Tequila are **distilled** alcohols.
- If a beverage contains at least 20% **Alcohol by Volume (ABV)**, it is called *spirit*. *Liquors* are similar to spirits. The

only difference is that liquors come with added sweetness and flavoring. Liquors and spirits, both are strong alcoholic beverages. The following are a few most popular alcoholic beverages –

Beverage	Process/ Raw Material	Origin	Alcohol by Volume (ABV in %)
Beer	Beer is obtained by fermenting liquid mixture of cereals such as corn, rye, wheat, barley and yeast.	Throughout the world.	5 – 10
Brandy	Brandy is obtained by distilling the fermented fruit juices.		40 – 50
Gin	Gin is obtained by distilling the fermented juice of Juniper berries with water.	Holland	40 – 50
Rum	Rum is obtained by fermenting Sugarcane juice or Molasses for at least three years.	Central/ South America	40 – 55
Tequila	Tequila is obtained by distilling fermented juices of Blue Agave plants.	Mexico	40 - 50
Vodka	Vodka is prepared by distilling starch or sugar-rich plant matter.	Russia	35 - 50
Whisky	Whisky is prepared by distilling fermented juice of cereal grains.	Scotland	40 - 55

Wines	Wines are obtained from fruits such as grapes, peaches, plums, apricots, pomegranate. The fruits are crushed and fermented in large containers.	France/ South Africa/India	5 - 20

- Due to the unwanted side effects of alcohol on consumer and the society, it is the responsibility of food and beverage service staff to verify the young customer's age before serving alcoholic beverages.
- The equipment forms an inevitable part of food and beverage service. It plays an important role to build the mood of the guests, to complement the outlet theme, and to elevate guest experience. Right from the largest commodities used for food preparation and interior decoration such as chandeliers or ovens to the smallest piece of cutlery, furniture, or linen participate in creating overall ambience of the outlet.
- Let us discuss in detail the equipment used in food and beverage services –
- Furniture in F&B Services
- Furniture is an important part of any F&B Services outlet. It needs to be strong, easy to use and clean. The furniture plays an important role in bringing the look and creating an ambience of the outlet. The furniture, fixtures, and fittings are fixed commodities.
- Indoor Furniture
- It mainly consists of tables, chairs, push-down chairs, racks, and lockers.
- Outdoor Furniture
- It needs to be sturdy as well as attractive. It includes coffee tables and chairs, bar chairs, dining sets, day beds, loungers, hammocks, and swings.
- Fixtures and Fittings

- A **fixture** is any item bolted to the floor or walls. For example, air conditioners, electric plugs, sinks and toilets, art pieces, and television screens mounted on wall are fixtures.
- A **fitting** is any free standing item or an item that can be hung by a nail or hook. For example, paintings, mirrors, curtain rails, and lamps are fittings.
- Tableware in F&B Services
- Tableware consists of crockery, cutlery, glassware and linen used while serving and eating meals at a table. These are circulating equipment which can be grouped into the following types –
- Chinaware
- This is a collection of fine dishes, bowls, food platters, section dishes, ramekins, cups and saucers, soup spoons, vases, and ash trays made using a translucent ceramic material.
- Hollowware
- This consists of containers such as serving bowls, pots, kettles, ice jugs, and water. These containers are either made from glass or metals such as copper, brass, or stainless steel.
- Glassware
- This consists of articles made of fine glass. Glassware includes jugs, pitchers, drinkware, ash trays, vases, and similar articles.
- Silverware
- The objects in silverware are made of Electro Plated Nickel Silver (EPNS). These are made from an alloy of brass, zinc, stainless steel or nickel with silver plating of 10 to 15 microns. Silverware includes spoons, forks, knives, hollowware, drinkware, tongs, ice bucket, and a salver.
- Chaffing Dishes (Chafers)
- These are food warming dishes. They keep the food warm for an adequate time and temperature. They come in two variants: electric or chafer fuel candle.

- Chaffing dishes are available in multiple sizes, shapes, and lids. Modern-day chafing dishes are made of light metal or ceramic with handles, sometimes covered with a see-through lid.

Cutlery comprises of any hand-held implement for eating or serving food. It includes various spoons, forks, knives, and tongs. It is also called silverware or flatware. Cutlery is made of metals like stainless steel or silver.

In modern days, cutlery has come up in wonderful combinations — *spife* (spoon + knife), *spork* (spoon + fork), and *knork* (knife + fork).

Types of Spoons, Forks, and Knives

There are different types of spoons for serving or eating different kinds of food. The forks often accompany spoons or help independently to pick food bites. The knives are used to portion the food.

- **Dinner Spoon** (Table Spoon) – It has elongated round cup. It is used to eat main course food items. It can pick up just the right amount of rice, stew, or curry. It is always paired with a fork (with four tines) of the same length or a dessert knife.

- **Dessert Spoon, Dessert Knife, and Dessert Fork** – These are smaller than their main course peers and are used to have desserts.

- **Soup Spoon** – It has a round cup bigger than that of the table spoon. It is as long as a dinner spoon.

- **Tea/Coffee Spoons** – These are smaller than the dessert spoon in length and size of cup. We use these spoons to stir tea or coffee.

- **Sugar Spoon** – It has a flower shaped round cup. It is used to take sugar from sugar bowl of tea set.

- **Ice Cream Spoon** – It is a small spoon with flat rim that can help to cut the right amount of ice cream. It can come in small, medium, and large sizes according to the quantity of the ice cream served and the size of the bowl.

- **Cocktail (Soda) Spoon** – It is a drink spoon with a long handle that helps the spoon to reach the bottom of a tall glass.

- **Butter knife** – It has short rectangular blade that is sharp on the lower side to form an edge. It is useful in cutting semi-firm pieces of butter and apply them on food items such as breads.

- **Salad Spoon** – It is always used in pair with salad fork. It helps mixing and serving salad efficiently.
- **Serving Spoon** – It is a spoon with large round cup designed to serve stews and rice.

- **Deli (Fruit) Fork** – has two tines. It helps to pick thinly sliced food such as slices of fruits.
- **Roast Fork** – It is the largest fork. It has longer and stronger tines that help to hold and pick large meat or vegetable pieces.
- **Cake Knife** – It is a flat, elongated triangle-shaped knife and is used to cut pieces of cake and handle it smoothly.

Types of Glasses

The glasses and tumblers come in a wide variety of shapes and sizes. They are either footed with stem or non-footed. They can also be high-ball or low-ball. Some of the widely used shapes are –

- **Cooler** – It is used to serve welcome drinks or appetizers.
- **Flute** – It is a glass with a long cup and is mainly used to serve champagne.

- **Goblet** – It is a round glass with or without stem. The goblets with stem are used to serve wines and brandy. A non-footed version is used to serve whisky.
- **Margarita** – It is a variant of goblet with a wide round dish-like cup. Margarita is used as a cocktail, mocktail, or a sorbet glass.
- **Mug** – It is used to serve beers.
- **Nonic Glass** – It is a tall glass with a broad rim. It is used to serve beers.
- **Pilsner** – It is a high-ball glass used to serve cold coffee, iced tea, juices, and beer. A pilsner can support beers or aerated drinks gracefully.
- **Pint** – It is a glass used to pour distilled alcohol into other glasses.
- **Shot Glass** – It is a small glass used to consume fermented or distilled alcohol directly. It can also be used to pour distilled alcohol into other glasses for mixing with water or sparkling water.
- **Snifter** – It is used to serve spirits.
- **Thistle Glass** – Its silhouette is shaped like a thistle flower. These glasses have tapered broad rims with round cups attached to a stem and disk. It is used to serve ales and aerated drinks.
- **Tulip Glass** – It is used to serve beer, cocktail, or mocktail.

Housekeeping – Definition, Role, Responsibilities and Layout

The housekeeping department is an essential component of any hospitality establishment. It is responsible for maintaining the cleanliness, tidiness, and hygiene of the entire property, including guest rooms, public areas, and back-of-house spaces. The primary goal of the housekeeping team is to ensure that guests have a comfortable, safe, and enjoyable stay by providing them with a clean and well-maintained environment.

The housekeeping department typically consists of a team of dedicated professionals who are trained to perform a wide range of tasks, including cleaning, laundry, room setup, and guest services. They work closely with other departments, such as the front office and maintenance, to ensure that all guest requests are handled promptly and efficiently.

In addition to maintaining the physical appearance of the property, the housekeeping department also plays a critical role in ensuring compliance with health and safety regulations. They are responsible for implementing procedures and protocols that help prevent the spread of infectious diseases, such as COVID-19, and other health hazards.

1. Definition of Housekeeping

Housekeeping may be defined as the 'provision of a clean, comfortable, safe and aesthetically appealing environment'. By another definition, 'housekeeping is an operational department in a hotel, which is responsible for cleanliness, maintenance, aesthetic upkeep of rooms, public areas, back areas, and the surroundings'.

The term Housekeeping outside the hospitality, hospital refers to the management of daily duties and chores involved in the running of a household, such as cleaning, cooking, home maintenance, shopping, and bill payment, etc. These daily recurring tasks may be performed by any members of the household, or by other persons like butlers or maids who are hired for the purpose.

2. Role of Housekeeping

The housekeeping department in the hotel ensures the cleanliness, maintenance, and aesthetic appeal of all rooms and public areas. The housekeeping department not only turnarounds (prepares and cleans guestrooms) promptly it also cleans and maintains everything in the hotel so that the property is as fresh and attractive similar to the day when it opened the doors for the business.

The effort that the housekeeping makes in giving a guest a desirable room has a direct bearing on the guest's experience in a hotel. More employees are working in the housekeeping department when compared to any other hotel department.

Being responsible for the turnaround of the rooms promptly, housekeeping's primary communications are with the front desk/reception team. Each room status is updated regularly from the housekeeping to the front desk and vice versa. With new technologies available a room status update can be done via the hotel software, telephone systems, housekeeping mobile applications, etc.

Housekeeping also coordinates closely with the maintenance or engineering department, as the housekeeping staff identifies different types of maintenance issues while cleaning the rooms and reports to the maintenance team for rectification or replacement. Example snags or issues with the TV, AC, Heating unit, Plumbing, Lighting, Electrical faults, Furniture, Toilet, Vanity, Tub, towel racks, Ventilation issues, etc.

The role of housekeeping can change depending upon the type or category of the hotel, for example, only in a luxury or full-service hotel evening or turndown services are offered by the housekeeping department. The housekeeping department is one of the major '*Support Centre*' in the hotel as it doesn't generate any major revenue for the hotel.

Housekeeping is considered a '*back of the house*' department even though they have some direct contact with the guests; for example, while cleaning rooms, picking up laundry, providing evening or turn down services, etc.

3. Housekeeping Department Organizational Chart

The housekeeping organizational chart provides a clear picture of the line of authority, The housekeeping department in a large hotel or 5 Star Hotel is headed by the executive housekeeper. They report to the general manager, the resident manager, or the rooms division manager in a large hotel. In the case of a chain of hotels, the executive housekeeper also reports to the director of housekeeping, who heads the housekeeping departments in all the hotels of that chain. The deputy housekeeper assists the executive housekeeper and looks after the various areas of responsibility in the hotel, that is, floors, public areas, the linen room, desk control and staffing, etc.

The Housekeeping Organizational Chart in a large hotel also contains multiple supervisors for each section of the housekeeping like the laundry, Desk Control, Floor Supervisor, Public Area Supervisor, Night Supervisor, etc. Each of these supervisors reports to the assistant housekeeper or the Executive housekeeper.

4. Different Sections in the Housekeeping

Executive Housekeeper's office: An Executive housekeeper has to plan, counsel, brief and meet her subordinates. It should preferably be a glass-panelled office to give her/him a view of what is happening outside the office. The office should be led by a cabin for the secretary who would control movement into the housekeeper's office.

Desk control room: This room acts as a nerve system center for coordination and communication with the front office and other departments. The desk control room should have a large notice board to pin up staff schedules and day-to-day instructions. The desk control room is the point where all staff report for duty and check out at the duty end.

Linen room: This is the room where current linens are stored for issue and receipt. The room should be large airy and free from heat and humidity. It should have adequate shelves, easily accessible to stack all linen. It should be secured and offer no possibility of pilferage. The linen room should have a counter, across which the exchange of linen takes place. The room should preferably be adjoining the laundry to supply linen to and from the laundry.

Linen room store: This room stores the stock of new linen & cloth materials for uniforms, etc. The stock maintained should be enough to replenish the whole hotel at a time. However, these stocks are only touched when the current linen in circulation falls short due to shortage, damage, or loss. The room should be cool and dry with ample shelves, generally 6" above the ground.

Uniform room: This room stocks the uniform for urgent use. Smaller hotels may choose to combine the uniform room with the linen room. A separate uniform room depends upon the volume of uniforms in circulation. The only difference will be that the uniform room would have adequate hanging facilities as many uniforms are best maintained when hung.

Tailor's room: This room is kept for house tailors who attend to the stitching and patch-up work of linen and uniforms. Room is avoided if the mending and the stitching jobs are done on a contract basis.

Lost and Found section: This section should be small and airy with cupboards to store guest articles lost and maybe claimed later.

Flower room: This should be an air-conditioned room to keep flowers fresh. The room should have a work table, a sink with a water supply, and all the necessary tools required for flower arrangement.

Laundry: This is an important section under housekeeping which is responsible for the cleaning of all fabrics used in the hotel. The section should be adjacent to the linen room to avoid excessive steps. Laundry should ensure the cleanness and drying of all guest clothes, employee uniforms, and linen to the best-assured standard.

Main Responsibilities of Housekeeping

- To ensure well-furnished and maintained guestrooms and public areas.
- To ensure excellence in housekeeping sanitation, safety, comfort, and aesthetics for hotel guests.
- To oversee the coordination of and administer all housekeeping programs and projects.
- To act as a source of contact in interdepartmental communications, vendors, professional agencies, etc.
- To provide a budget, budget control, and forecasting related to housekeeping.
- To achieve the maximum efficiency in ensuring the care and comfort of guests & in the smooth functioning of the department.

- To establish a welcoming atmosphere.
- To ensure courteousness, and reliable service from all staff to the guest.
- To ensure a high standard of cleanliness and general upkeep in all areas for which the department is responsible.
- To provide linen in rooms, restaurants, banquet halls, conference halls, health clubs, etc, as well as to maintain an inventory for the same.
- To provide uniforms for all the staff & maintain inventory for the same.
- To Cater to the laundering requirements of hotel linen, staff uniforms, and guests.
- To provide & maintain the floral decorations and to maintain the landscaped areas of the hotel.
- To select the right contractors & ensure the quality of work is maintained.
- To co-ordinate renovation and refurnishing of the property in consultation with the management & interior designers.
- Coordinate with the purchasing department for the procurement of guest supplies, cleaning agents, equipment, fabrics, carpets, & other items used in the hotel.
- To deal with lost & found articles.
- Carpet shampooing and maintenance.
- Dealing with any guest queries, complaints & requests as they occur.
- To keep the general manager or administrator informed of all matters requiring attention.

Standard Room Status Codes Used in Housekeeping

Occupied: A guest currently registered to the room.

Complimentary: The room is occupied, but the guest is not charged for its use.

Stayover: The guest is not checking out today and will remain at least one more night.

On-change: The guest has departed, but the room has not yet been cleaned and readied for resale.

Do Not Disturb (DND): The guest has requested not to be disturbed.

Sleep-out: A guest was booked into the room, but the bed has not been used.

Skipper: The guest left the hotel without paying the bill.

Sleeper: The guest has settled his/her account and left the hotel, but the front office staff has failed to properly update the room's status.

Vacant and ready: The room has been cleaned and inspected and is ready for an arriving guest.

Out Of Order (OOO): The cannot be assigned to a guest and is blocked for maintenance activity.

Lock Out: The room has been locked so that the guest cannot re-enter until they are cleared by the front desk.

DNCO: Did not check out, the guest made arrangements to settle his or her account but left without informing the front desk.

Due Out: The room is expected to become vacant after the following day's check-out time.

Check Out: The guest has settled his or her account, returned the room keys, and left the hotel.

Late Checkout: The guest has requested and is being allowed to check out later than the standard check-out time.

Early Check-in: The guest has requested and is being allowed to check in earlier than the standard check-in time.

Cleaning Equipment Used in Housekeeping

Efficient cleaning and maintenance are dependent upon high-quality cleaning equipment, correctly used. Though only 5-10% of the overall cost incurred on cleaning is accounted for by cleaning equipment and agents, selecting the ideal equipment plays a major role in the cleaning process. There will often be several ways of carrying out any particular cleaning task and different types of equipment that can be employed for it.

It is the executive housekeeper's responsibility to select the most appropriate piece of equipment according to the hotel's requirements. Most types of cleaning equipment fall under the category of recycled items, but a few large pieces of items may be considered fixed assets. The correct choice of quality cleaning equipment could save costs due to breakdowns, reduce fatigue, and ensure overall efficiency in operations.

The equipment used in the cleaning of the surface, furniture, and fittings in a hotel building includes both 1) **Manual equipment** and 2) **Mechanical Equipment.**

1. Manual Equipment: Manual equipment can include all types of equipment that clean or aid in the cleaning process by directly using the manoeuvre, operation, and energy of employees. Examples of Manual cleaning equipment are Brushes, Mops, Brooms, Cloths, Polish applicators, Containers, Buckets, etc.

2. Mechanical Equipment: The various pieces of mechanical equipment used in the housekeeping department are usually powered by electricity or gas. The staff should be well-trained in the operation of this equipment since incorrect usage will not only lead to inefficient cleaning but may also become a safety hazard. Examples of mechanical equipment used in housekeeping are Vacuum cleaners, Electric brooms, Wet-and-dry vacuum cleaners, floor maintenance machines for scrubbing, buffing polishing, etc.

The following areas constitute the layout of a housekeeping department:

- Executive housekeeper's cabin
- Secretary's cabin
- Desk Control Room
- Lost and Found Section
- Housekeeping Stores
- Florist's room
- Linen and Uniform room
- Linen Store
- Sewing room
- Floor Pantry/Maid's service room

- Overall, the housekeeping department is a vital part of any hospitality operation, and its success is essential to the overall guest experience. A well-trained, efficient, and professional housekeeping team can make all the difference in ensuring that guests feel welcome, comfortable, and satisfied throughout their stay.

Significance of Food Production Department & kitchen Planning in Hotel Industry

There is a new concept of Food production gaining the spotlight in the food and culinary Industry. Professional chefs often talk about the significance of Food production in the Hotel and Hospitality Industry. Let's understand the concept and role of the food production department in detail.

Food production involves the preparation of food where raw material is converted into ready-made food products. It's utilized either for Human use or for the food processing Industry.

There are different kinds of plants and animal products that become the source of human food. These include grains, pulses, spices, honey, milk and dairy products, vegetables, egg, meat, fish, and much more. Several kinds of food production methods include chopping and slicing vegetables, food fermentation, boiling, frying, grilling, mixing, fruit juice processing, steaming, preserving, packaging, etc.

So, the food production department is responsible for food preparation in a hotel, restaurant, or hospitality industry. As a career, the scope of food production is increasing in India as well as the world. The guests who stay in a hotel or walk in a restaurant come to enjoy the meals.

The sub-departments in a food production department are:

1. **Main Kitchen**– It's a large kitchen area for the preparation of food in Food and beverage outlets. There are further subsections in the main kitchen that include Indian section, Continental section, South Indian Section, Tandoori.

2. **Pantry**– The majority of orders in the pantry section are tea/coffee, salads, raita, sandwiches that operate 24/7.

3. **Bakery and Confectionary**– It serves baked items like Cakes, Pastries, Muffins, Chocolates, etc.

4. **Butchery**– In this section, all meat supplies are received, cleaned, and stored.

5. **Banquet section**– The large-scale cooking for functions takes place in the Banquet section.
6. **Chefs area**– All the executive chefs sit together and make menu planning.
7. **Commisisonary**– In this section, all the green vegetables are stored in bulk.
8. **Walkins**– Based on the Size of the hotel, there are at least 2 to 3 walk-in refrigerators and one particular to store meat.

Introduction to the Professional Concept of Kitchen:

In common terms, Kitchen is a place where food is cooked and it has equipment that is used in the processing of cooking. At the same time, a chef is a person tasked with managing the kitchen and cooking. The Kitchen includes several units of food production from cultivation to waste management.

The different kinds of the kitchen include:-

(1). Main kitchen- Main Kitchen or central kitchen is the conventional kitchen that is usually located in the center of a restaurant. It occupies a large space and has multiple sections. It provides a wide range of food varieties Indian, Continental, Mexican, Italian, etc. There is a hierarchy of chefs working in the main kitchen. The main kitchen is made adjacent to a pantry, bakery, and commissary.

(2). Satellite Kitchen- Satellite Kitchen is constructed for a particular outlet where it is not possible to set up the main kitchen for location issues. It's an important asset for specialty restaurants like Chinese, Nepalese, Continental, etc that are separated from the main kitchen.

(3). Fast food kitchen- The concept of fast food kitchen is inspired by American Catering technology. Mostly, it provides dry and light food. It's located in a public area where food is taken away and consumed. A fast-food kitchen is common at airports, railway stations, roadside service complexes, etc.

(4). Display kitchen- The food is prepared and cooked in a full open view of customers in the Display kitchen. This kind of kitchen appeals to the eyes, plating is lucrative, and adds to the dining experience of the guests. Also, the pleasant aroma and simple fresh cooking become a source of attraction for the customers.

(5). Experimental kitchen- The objective behind an experimental kitchen is different from a conventional kitchen. It has the task of improving food production instead of serving the guests. Experimental Kitchen researches and develops new food items for the menu.

Executive Chef makes its staff equipped with kitchen planning skills for preparing them to take up professional roles in the F & B Industry. There are expert educators, theory classes, and practical workshops for students in different courses to gain a thorough knowledge of kitchen Management in the hospitality industry.

Kitchen planning is a vital aspect of F & B and hospitality outlets. Kitchen planning or kitchen layout is designed to ensure that the staff can move freely without any fatigue or accident. Furthermore, it ensures smooth and efficient workflow with the timely pickup of food.

A good kitchen should save time and effort, ensure easy supervision, should have an efficient workflow and sufficient workplace to work safely.

Duties and Responsibilities of Food Production Department

It will be right to say that kitchen is the heart of a hotel; just like the pumps our blood to all the parts of the body, kitchen supplies food to all the parts of the kitchen. So in this statement you can understand that how is Food Production important in any hotel.

There are some importance of this department includes in hotel –

Responsible for creating the guest experience – The food that is served to guests is a major part of their overall experience at a hotel. If the food is not good, it can leave a negative impression on guests and make them less likely to stay at the hotel again.

Generate a significant amount of revenue – The food production department is often one of the most profitable departments in a hotel. This is because guests are often willing to pay a premium for good food.

Help to attract and retain guests – Guests are more likely to stay at a hotel that has a good reputation for its food. The food production department can help to attract new guests and keep existing guests coming back.

It can help to improve the hotel's image – A hotel with a good reputation for its food is seen as a more luxurious and upscale hotel. This can help to attract new guests and improve the hotel's overall image.

Objectives of Food Production in Hotel

The objectives of food production in a hotel can vary depending on the specific hotel, but some common objectives include in my point of view are:

To provide guests with high-quality, delicious food

This is the most important objective of any food production department. Guests expect to be served good food when they stay at a hotel, and the food production department is responsible for meeting or exceeding those expectations.

Maintain a high level of food safety

Food safety is essential in any food service operation, but it is especially important in a hotel where guests are paying for their meals. The food production department must take all necessary precautions to ensure that the food they serve is safe to eat.

To operate efficiently and cost-effectively

The food production department must be able to produce food in a timely and efficient manner without sacrificing quality. They must also be able to control costs in order to keep food prices affordable for guests.

To create a positive work environment for staff

The food production department is a busy and demanding environment, but it is important to create a positive work environment for staff. This will help to ensure that staff are motivated and productive, and that they are able to provide guests with the best possible service.

Duties and Responsibilities of Food ProductionDepartment

The food production department is responsible for the preparation, cooking, and presentation of food in a restaurant, hotel, or other foodservice establishment. The specific responsibilities of the department vary depending on the size and type of establishment, but they typically include the following:

Purchasing and receiving food – It responsible for ordering and receiving food from suppliers. They must ensure that the food is fresh, of high quality, and meets the establishment's specifications.

Storage and inventory – Responsible for storing food in a safe and sanitary manner. They must also keep track of inventory levels to ensure that there is always enough food on hand to meet customer demand.

Preparation of Food – There is no hard and easy rule the department prepare the food according to recipes and established standards. This may involve cutting, chopping, slicing, dicing, cooking, baking, or frying food.

Cooking – The food production is responsible for cooking food to ensure that it is safe to eat and that it meets the establishment's standards of quality.

Presentation – Making a food is different but how we demonstrate the food to a guest that is impress more so this department responsible for presenting food in a visually appealing way. This may involve garnishing dishes, plating food, or arranging food on a buffet table.

Sanitation – The food production department is responsible for maintaining a sanitary environment in the kitchen. This includes cleaning and sanitizing equipment, utensils, and surfaces on a regular basis.

Safety – Responsible for ensuring the safety of employees and customers. This includes following all safety procedures, such as using proper personal protective equipment and handling food safely.

In addition to these responsibilities, the food production department may also be responsible for other tasks, such as:

- Training employees
- Developing recipes
- Menu planning
- Cost control

Printed in the USA
CPSIA information can be obtained
at www.ICGtesting.com
LVHW041924090924
790538LV00012B/562